THE
COMPASSIONATE
GEEK®

THE
COMPASSIONATE
GEEK®

HOW ENGINEERS, IT PROS AND OTHER TECH SPECIALISTS CAN MASTER HUMAN RELATIONS SKILLS TO DELIVER OUTSTANDING CUSTOMER SERVICE

THIRD EDITION

DON R. CRAWLEY

Auburn, Washington
CompassionateGeek.com

For more information about special discounts for bulk purchases, please contact:

On the web: *CompassionateGeek.com*
On the phone: (206) 988-5858
Email: info@compassionategeek.com

Editor: Henry Covey, Cogitate Studio, Portland, Oregon
Cover design by Jason Sprenger, Overland Park, Kansas, *www.fourthcup.org*

Library of Congress Control Number: 2013915178
ISBN-13: 978-0-9836607-3-6

Compassionate Geek
Auburn, WA
United States of America

To Janet

"Technology, like art, is a soaring exercise of the human imagination."

—Daniel Bell
The Winding Passage

CONTENTS

CHAPTER THREE

CHAPTER FOUR

CHAPTER EIGHT

CHAPTER NINE

WATCH THE VIDEO: HOW IT PROS CAN

MASTER HUMAN RELATIONS SKILLS

Watch my video on *How IT Pros Can Master Human Relations Skills to Deliver Outstanding Customer Service* on my video channel at *www.doncrawley.com/videos*.

Technology, like art, is a soaring exercise of the human imagination, wrote Daniel Bell (1919–2011), a widely-respected American sociologist of the twentieth century. (Bell 1980) Bell's quote reminds those of us who work in technical fields that ours is, in fact, the practice of an art.

So why should we care about customer service? Why be a compassionate geek? In a nutshell, by providing great customer service, we develop a relationship of trust and respect with our end users. They learn to come to us early, when problems are small, so we don't have to expend additional resources later putting out big fires. Our users work better, too. They're more productive, creative, and efficient. They speak well of us behind our backs. It's a positive feedback loop that's good for everyone.

The art of what we do lies in the creative technical solutions we design to solve perplexing human problems. In fact, our work is less about technology than about helping our end users and customers have a better experience and work more productively, creatively, and efficiently. Even if you're a coder who never has to directly interact with end users, your work exists ultimately because it helps another human being, maybe even yourself. Perhaps cliché, but the old statement is true that we wouldn't have a job if it weren't for our end users or customers. If we fail to create a good experience for them, they'll quit asking for our help.

There are times when that may sound good to you, but consider this: If they don't ask for our help, several things can happen, none of them good:

- The end user might decide to try to solve the problem him or herself. Sure, sometimes this works, but other times it can be disastrous if a user starts tinkering without knowing what he or she is doing.

- The customer or end user might give up on learning new technologies that could help her or him do a better job.

- A computer network user might engage in unsafe, non-secure practices that could jeopardize your entire network.

- We might experience what I call, "death by water cooler," where users and customers start bad-mouthing us behind our backs. This can torpedo careers, lead to outsourcing, or at the least, create reputation problems that can be difficult to repair.

Month after month, I read reports from research companies saying that companies are searching for IT people with good people skills, often in response to complaints from frustrated end users and customers. Really, our objective, not only in the context of customer service, but in every aspect of our work, should be to create a positive outcome for our end user or customer, our organization, and ourselves.

Most of us who work in technical fields have vast sums of knowledge of the technical components of our world. It's the human element that poses the greatest challenge for us. Unpredictable, confounding, emotional, at once both brilliant and clueless, our fellow humans can make the most complicated programming puzzle or other engineering challenge seem trivial by comparison.

This book is for any technical professional who wants to master the most difficult part of any technical job: working with the end user.

In the pages to come, you'll find practical concepts, tips, and techniques based on my years of experience in information systems and technology, current sociological and neurological research, and working all over the world with all kinds of people. I've also included several interactive exercises to help you solidify some of the concepts, gain insights into your present point-of-view, and start the process of change. The goal is for you to actually use this book.

Be careful not to get caught up in the "yeah, buts." This is where someone needs help, seeks the guidance of a trusted counselor or mentor, and when the counselor offers suggestions, the person seeking help says, "Yeah, but that won't work for me," or similar words.

The other undermining mindset I see frequently is the "theys." This is the person who looks externally for solutions rather than internally. You'll hear phrases like "They won't do that" or "They don't understand." I recently gave a talk on customer service where one of the attendees, a seasoned mainframe and Unix administrator, was busy blaming everyone but herself for her problems.

There's no doubt that we sometimes have to work with unsavory, disagreeable, or incompetent individuals. One of my favorite quotes is from the Reverend R. Robert Cueni who once joked in a sermon, "All the world's problems would be solved if I just ran things." How many of us feel that way from time-to-time? The reality is that we can't change other people. Let go of any ideas you may have about changing other people We can only change ourselves. As perfect as we are, if we're not getting the reaction we want from other people, we need to start by looking in the mirror. If you're not getting the response you want from other people, focus on changing yourself and how you interact with them. This is the first key to success.

People skills can be learned. Really.

Remember, too, to grant yourself the grace to be human. That means you're subject to the bane of our species, human frailty. You're not always going to do things right. Just keep practicing! Lasting change usually comes in small increments over time. It will come. If you're having difficulty, sometimes it can be helpful to find a mentor, someone you respect and who gets along well with people. Just ask for his or her assistance.

However you choose to approach it, whether by yourself, with a mentor, or in a group, there are tangible benefits to learning the art of human relations and outstanding customer service in terms of your career, your health, and your happiness. Just know that this is a lifelong journey with some setbacks and lots of surprises, so jump in and enjoy the ride!

ACKNOWLEDGMENTS

This book traces its roots to a request from the State of Washington to develop a customer service workshop for IT staff. With the assistance of Paul Senness and Peggy Jacobson, I developed the courseware and presented the workshop. Word spread, and soon my company was presenting the workshop to other clients and continuing to develop new materials. After receiving several requests, I wrote the early editions of this book.

Thanks to Janet, my wife, and the rest of my family, to editor Henry Covey, artist Jason Sprenger, to Michael Phillips and Alexis Dane, and all of the IT folks who understand the importance of the delighted end user.

A SPECIAL ACKNOWLEDGEMENT

Every book is a product of the combined efforts of many people. This book would not have been possible without the writing, mentoring, commiseration, intellectual challenges, mental health and spiritual (and spirits) counseling, and friendship of Paul Senness.

Thanks, Paul.

com·pas·sion (kəm-'păsh-ən), *n.*, Profound awareness of another's suffering combined with the desire to alleviate it.

geek (gēk), slang, *n.*, A term of pride referring to a computer or other technical expert

CHAPTER ONE

THE FOUNDATIONS OF SERVICE

"People will forget what you say, they will forget what you do,
but they never will forget how you make them feel."

—Dr. Maya Angelou

INTERACTIVE EXERCISE:
Remembering the Good, the Bad, and the Awful

This exercise is designed to help you recall both good and bad technical support situations in which you were the one receiving customer support. You'll need a blank sheet of paper. On the paper, draw a line down the middle to create two columns. At the top of the left column, put "Heroes," and at the top of the right column, put "Villains."

Now, reflect on times when you called a company for technical support, visited the customer service counter in a store, tried to return an item you had purchased, or in some other way interacted with the customer relations arm of some company. It doesn't have to be related to technical support either. In the column labeled "Heroes," write two or three incidents in which you felt you received excellent support. In the column labeled "Villains," write down two or three incidents in which you felt you received really bad support. In both columns, write down what was happening that made it a good or bad experience, what was being said and/or done, and how you felt during the experience. (You might want to use a separate sheet of paper for this exercise. We'll be referring to it later on.)

Now, stop and think about the actions of the heroes and the actions of the villains. Think, also, about the things you do when supporting end users or customers. Are your actions closer to those of your heroes or your villains? Be honest with yourself about this!

As you read through the rest of the book, reflect back on your comments. Think about what makes for a great support session, what makes for a poor support session, and about your own experiences, both good and bad, providing support as an IT support professional or customer service representative.

Our objective is to make our end users and customers' experiences with us more closely aligned with those in the heroes column and to, hopefully, never have people describe their interaction with us as that of a villain.

THE TRAITS OF THE MASTERS

Chances are your competitors sell products and services that are quite similar to yours; they may even be similarly priced. Oftentimes, what makes a difference to your users and customers is their experience: how you make them feel.

Everybody talks about customer service, and lots of people teach customer service, but I began to wonder if there might be some foundational skills that could guide people in serving their end users and customers. As a trainer and consultant working with organizations and industries as diverse as Facebook, state government, healthcare, universities, and financial services, I observed that within every organization, there are usually key individuals who simply "get it," the ones end users and customers always go back to if given a choice, not only when they have problems, but for every type of interaction with the organization. As I observed those individuals in my seminars and workshops, I began to see common traits emerge. In addition to technical skills, those individuals also show four particular skills in dealing with people. This section is about those traits. If you can master the four skills described in this section, the rest of your work in learning great customer service will naturally fall into place, and perhaps not surprisingly, these four skills are also the qualities of being a great human being.

To do this, we take closer at those people who "get it," as well as those who don't.

BONUS VIDEO: THE FOUR TRAITS OF
THE CUSTOMER SERVICE MASTERS

Watch my video on *The Four Traits of the Customer Service Masters* on my video channel at *www.doncrawley.com/videos*.

SOUNDTHINKING POINT:

Technical Competency is Assumed

For the purpose of this discussion, your technical competency is assumed. Without technical competency, all the human relations skills in the world won't matter. You simply must know the products and services you support in and out. As much as possible, use them in your daily life. Experiment with them in a lab or test-bed environment. Break them, fix them, test solutions, read about them, take workshops on them, and generally try to experience the products you support the same way your customers or end users experience them. Strive to know more about the products and services you support than anyone else in the world.

Something Intrinsic

After observing and training so many people in customer service situations over the years, it seems that there are really four traits, **intrinsic** qualities, that are common to the "hero type," those individuals who, even without training, simply seem to know how to deal effectively with their users and customers.

#1: COMPASSION

"Compassion is the antitoxin of the soul: where there is compassion even the most poisonous impulses remain relatively harmless."

—Eric Hoffer

The first trait is **compassion**, the act of caring about the well-being of another. It really boils down to the timeless wisdom of the Golden Rule: Treat others the way you would have them treat you.

Another way to think of compassion in customer service is, "Doing it with heart."

Compassion is about one human relating to another human. When our users and customers place themselves in our care, they are first and foremost a human being. We may not like their political views or the way they look or act. Frankly, we may not like anything about them, but they are still human beings deserving of our human-to-human care, understanding, and respect.

Herndon Hasty was one of the best bosses I ever had. Once, when we'd gone to lunch together, I came out of the restaurant after him and saw him feeding strangers' parking meters. He didn't know I saw him. There was nothing in it for him other than a good feeling; it was simply an act of kindness. When I wrote to him asking if I could mention him by name in my book, he told me about his latest thing which is leaving iced water for the refuse collection staff on hot summer days. Herndon's focus is on making the experience of living better for everyone around him.

When you genuinely care about what happens to other people, you instinctively look for ways to better their experience.

EXERCISE:

Learning How to Be More Compassionate

I believe that most of us are compassionate by nature. Sometimes, when we get in a hurry or when we're facing troubles of our own, we may not act as compassionately as we do at other times.

Here are three tips to help you learn how to be consistently compassionate:

1. Use the "just like me" concept. That's where, when you meet someone new, you say to yourself, "Just like me, this person (is seeking happiness, is trying to avoid pain and suffering, has experienced sadness and loneliness, is learning about life). (Palmer 1997) Think of this as finding the common ground you share with another human. No matter who you are or who the other person is, there is common ground. Certainly, we share more common ground with some people than with others, but that's not the point. You may have heard someone say, "We're all the same, deep down inside." I don't believe that's true, and that's not the point, either. The point is this: there are some things that are common to all human experiences. The person striving to be compassionate will look for the experiences, needs, and desires shared with other humans.

2. Stop focusing so much on yourself. Think about the other person's needs from his or her perspective, not your own.

3. Slow down. In a famous 1973 experiment at Princeton Theological Seminary, a group of forty seminary students were recruited and then assigned to give talks on a variety of subjects, including the Biblical parable of The Good Samaritan. The experimenters had the budding theologians start in one building but then sent them to a separate building to give their talk. Between the two buildings, the researchers had stationed a shabbily dressed man who appeared to be in pain.

The point of the experiment was to see which of the students would stop and offer assistance, like the Samaritan, and which would pass by without offering assistance, like the priest and the Levite of the parable. (Luke n.d.) It turned out that the students in the greatest hurry were least likely to offer assistance. (Darley and Batson 1973) In my own life, I've noticed that the times when I'm least compassionate are the times when I'm in the greatest hurry.

#2: EMPATHY

*"Taught by time, my heart has learned to glow for other's good,
and melt at other's woe."*

—Homer

The second of those traits is **empathy**, closely related to compassion. Empathy is the ability to connect with another individual emotionally, to feel what they're feeling. It's often known as "putting yourself in someone else's shoes" or "walking a mile in another's shoes." In my customer service seminars and workshops, I recommend the use of empathetic phrases, such as:

- *"I'd feel that way, too, if it happened to me."*

- *"I don't blame you for feeling that way; I'd be as upset
  as you are in your position."*

- *"I can see how frustrated you are and I don't blame you."*

It's also important to be authentic and sincere in your empathy. If you simply can't relate to your user's situation, it's OK to say so when you combine it with human understanding. For example, suppose that your end user is a trial attorney who is in the midst of last-minute preparations for a jury summation in a murder trial when his computer crashes. Don't say you know how this person feels. That's like a man telling a woman he understands childbirth. Instead, you can say something to the end user like, "I'm so sorry that happened. I'm going to do everything I can to take care of it for you." Then, quietly go about solving the problem. In less high-pressure situations, you might say something like: "I've never been in your situation, so I'm not going to tell you I understand. I can't even imagine what that's like, but I am going to do everything within my power to help you. I'm sure if I were in your situation, I'd feel the same way you do." The key is sincere, human-to-human empathy.

EXERCISE:
Practicing Ways to Be More Empathetic

Here are four ways to practice being more empathetic:

1. Imagine how you would feel in the other person's situation. Imagine the range of emotions the other person must be experiencing at that moment.

2. Use empathetic phrases similar to those mentioned above, such as: "I know this is frustrating for you" and "I don't blame you and would feel that way, too, if I were in your position." It never hurts to offer a sincere expression of sympathy, such as "I'm sorry that happened to you."

3. Lose distractions. Close the book you're reading, turn off your monitor, leave your cell phone in your pocket or purse, even if it rings or notifies you of a new text message, and give the other person your full attention. Later in the book, I'll discuss how to be a better listener. Being a great listener is a great way to show sincere empathy.

4. When you're dealing with a person face-to-face, ensure your body language conveys empathy. Lean in to the other person (but don't get too close) and don't fidget or futz with other activities such as texting or Facebooking. Don't even look at your cell phone, not even a quick and subtle glance.

#3: LISTENING

"To be able to listen to others in a sympathetic and understanding manner is perhaps the most effective mechanism in the world for getting along with people and tying up their friendship for good."

—Unknown

"It is the province of knowledge to speak and it is the privilege of wisdom to listen."

—Oliver Wendell Holmes

The third trait is the ability to **listen**. This means that your sole focus is on what your user is saying. Later in the book, there's a complete chapter just on how to improve your listening skills. For now, just know that one of the greatest gifts one can give another is that of listening.

There are three stages to an effective listening process:

1. *Hearing.* This is the physical act of receiving sound vibrations and focusing your attention on the person speaking and the words he or she is saying.

2. *Understanding.* Understanding means you take the words you've heard and relate them to your own experiences and knowledge.

3. *Processing.* Processing is the act of taking what you understood the speaker to say and evaluating it.

A technique that can help you become a better listener is to listen as though you're going to be tested on what is being said. If you know there's a quiz coming up, you'll find a way to sharpen your focus on the speaker. Author and speaker Stephen Covey recommends repeating back what is said, using phrases like, "Let me make sure I understand. The problem is ... "

Three Tips for Being a Better Listener

In the listening chapter, I'll cover listening in greater depth. For now, here are three things you can do right away to be a better listener:

1. Listen as though there will be a test when the other person finishes speaking.

2. Stop talking, even silently in your mind. When you're talking, you can't listen.

3. Listen with the goal to understand what the other person means. Ask questions for clarification.

#4: RESPECT

"Respect for ourselves guides our morals, respect for others guides our manners."

—Laurence Sterne

"Respect a man, he will do the more."

—James Howell

The fourth essential skill is the ability to treat all people with **respect**, regardless of how you might feel about them. In fact, it's not necessary to respect someone to treat him or her with respect. Respecting someone is a matter of how you feel about that person and whether they have earned your respect. Treating someone with respect is a matter of your behavior and, frankly, is a reflection of how you feel about yourself. Certainly, people must earn our feelings of respect, but regardless of whether someone has earned it, all people should be treated with respect and dignity. It is a matter of your own dignity and character that you treat all things respectfully.

In the movie *The Green Mile*, Tom Hanks plays a death-row prison guard charged with guarding condemned convicts who had performed some terrible crimes. You could certainly argue that the men in his care were not deserving of respect, yet he treated them all respectfully. It may have been the first and only time in their lives when any of them were treated respectfully.

If we want to be treated with respect, we must model respectful behavior at every opportunity.

We must also respect ourselves and accept full responsibility for ourselves. We may not be in complete control of the things that happen to us, but we are in complete control of how we respond to those things. Examples of how we respect ourselves might include making respectful choices in the foods we eat, drinking water every day, avoiding destructive behaviors, and choosing friends and colleagues who are positive, up-lifting influences in our lives. It is a matter of being *intentional* in our behaviors. In other words, we *intend* to choose friends who are positive influences in our lives instead of simply befriending the first person who comes along. We can *intend* to eat foods that are nourishing for our bodies instead of simply eating whatever is available.

In our role as a service provider to people, we may find ourselves dealing with people we don't like or respect. We maintain our own dignity and self-respect when we treat all living things respectfully. In his landmark book, *Man's Search for Meaning*, author Viktor E. Frankl suggests that the true measure of an individual lies not in his or her usefulness, but in his or her ability to maintain a sense of dignity in all circumstances (Frankl 1959). It's easy to be arrogant and judgmental; it's more difficult and infinitely more meaningful to maintain your dignity in the face of undignified situations and people.

EXERCISE:

Treating People with Respect

*"We teach our children that everyone is entitled
to dignity and respect."*

—David E. Kelly

This is going to be a difficult exercise for many people. As I've tried to practice the following types of behaviors, I've found them very challenging. First, I'm going to describe some people and situations and have you think about how you might feel about them. Then, we'll go over some specific ways to treat them respectfully, regardless of how you feel about them or how they might treat you.

For the purpose of this exercise, assume that interventions by others, such as a company's human-relations officer or a police officer, are not available options. Also be careful about being condescending or disingenuous.

- You're walking on a sidewalk with your spouse or significant other. You're approached by a shabbily dressed man who asks for money. You don't believe in giving money to panhandlers. What do you say and do to maintain respect and dignity for you, your spouse, and the man asking for money?

- You're waiting in line for a drink at a coffee shop. The person next to you initiates small talk which turns into poisonous, slanderous comments about someone, perhaps a politician, whom you respect and admire. What do you say and do?

- You're a legal assistant in a law firm. A new client comes in who is accused of molesting a child. You have to meet with him or her to get a statement. What do you say and do?

- You're an atheist. Your company just hired someone who is a devout Christian and who praises Jesus at nearly every turn. What do you say and do?

- You're a devout Christian. Your company just hired someone who is an atheist and who mocks believers. What do you say and do?

These are difficult situations for anyone. How can you maintain your self-respect in such situations while also treating the other person with dignity and respect, even when you don't feel she or he is deserving of dignity and respect?

I think one of the keys to successfully navigating situations like those mentioned above is to focus on what YOU will do, not what you want the other person to do, nor how you feel about what they might have done. You can say to yourself, when dealing with an unsavory individual, that you're going to maintain your composure, self-respect, and dignity, no matter what the other does or did in the past.

SOUNDTHINKING POINT:
It's Really About Kindness

In a nutshell, the four traits of the customer service masters are about being kind. Ask yourself, as you interact with your fellow humans, "Am I being as kind as I possibly can be?"

THE PARADOXICAL COMMANDMENTS

In 1968, Dr. Kent M. Keith wrote the paradoxical commandments as part of a handbook for student leaders. They've been reprinted many times since then and falsely attributed to a variety of sources, including the Rev. Dr. Martin Luther King, Jr. and Mother Teresa. (In fact, Mother Teresa thought they were important enough to post on the wall of her children's home in Calcutta.) I met and spoke briefly with Dr. Keith at a National Speakers Association event in 2007. He's a humble man with a powerful message that certainly applies to our work in customer service and technical support. Here are the Paradoxical Commandments by Kent M. Keith:

1. People are illogical, unreasonable, and self-centered. Love them anyway.

2. If you do good, people will accuse you of selfish ulterior motives. Do good anyway.

3. If you are successful, you will win false friends and true enemies. Succeed anyway.

4. The good you do today will be forgotten tomorrow. Do good anyway.

5. Honesty and frankness make you vulnerable. Be honest and frank anyway.

6. The biggest men and women with the biggest ideas can be shot down by the smallest men and women with the smallest minds. Think big anyway.

7. People favor underdogs but follow only top dogs. Fight for a few underdogs anyway.

8. What you spend years building may be destroyed overnight. Build anyway.

9. People really need help but may attack you if you do help them. Help people anyway.

10. Give the world the best you have and you'll get kicked in the teeth. Give the world the best you have anyway.

© Copyright Kent M. Keith 1968, renewed 2001

The Paradoxical Commandments were written by Kent M. Keith as part of his book, *The Silent Revolution: Dynamic Leadership in the Student Council*, published in 1968 by Harvard Student Agencies, Cambridge, Massachusetts. More information is available at *www.paradoxicalcommandments.com*.

Competence/Charisma Continuum

As you can see from the preceding section on the traits of the customer service masters, two separate and distinct skill sets are required for a successful IT career: obviously, you must have outstanding technical skills, especially related to the product(s) you support, competence, and you must have an ability to understand, get along with, and influence people, charisma.

Think about all the people you know, both personally and from their public personas. Some of the people who come to mind probably have extremely high levels of technical competence and others less so, while some are very charismatic and others less so. In fact, we can divide people into four categories:

- Neither competent nor charismatic

- Charismatic but not competent

- Competent but not charismatic

- Competent and charismatic

Within these categories, people exist on a dynamic continuum where their levels of competency and charisma vary greatly from person to person. Not only that, the personal levels of competency and charisma within an individual can vary from moment to moment. Consider again the people you know. Generally, the least successful people, by most measures of success, display extremely low levels of both competency and charisma, and the opposite is true for those who show high levels of competency/charisma:

- **Neither competent nor charismatic**. Someone who dropped out of school, doesn't work, has a disagreeable personality, and always blames other people for his or her situation is an example of someone with extremely low levels of competency and charisma.

- **Charismatic, but not competent**. An example of someone who shows extremely high levels of charisma but has very little competency would be a con artist or a card cheat. (Admittedly, both con artists and card cheats require levels of competency, but not in a productive, honorable skill.)

- **Competent, but not charismatic**. Some people show extremely high levels of competency, but have limited people skills. An example of such a person might be someone who is a brilliant coder but has difficulty interacting successfully with other people. I worked with a radio station engineer once who was highly skilled in electrical engineering, but he was arrogant and quick to lose his temper. Even though he was technically competent, he was so difficult to work with that I had to find someone else to do his job.

- **Competent and charismatic**. The late Steve Jobs, co-founder of Apple Computer, was someone with high levels of both competence and charisma. Jobs is a great example, in fact, because he was not always likable, but he was very good at understanding people, gaining their respect, and persuading them to follow his lead.

Where are you on the continuum? To find out, look at the competency-charisma chart I've provided and rate yourself, where 1 equals virtually no competency/charisma, respectively, and 10 means you're the best there is in the entire world.

The Competency-Charisma Continuum

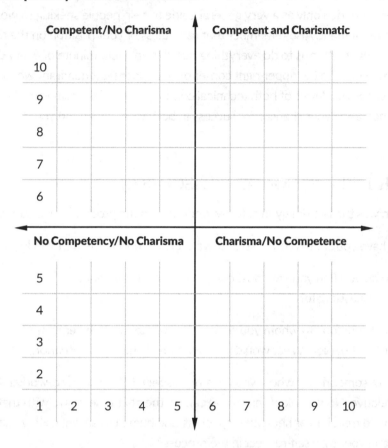

Each of us will land in different areas, based on differing levels of technical competence and people skills, but most fall somewhere toward the middle of the chart. Don't give any thought as to where your scores are compared to those of other people, however. (In our world, we love to compare ourselves to other people, but that's a really bad idea. Don't do it, ever!)

Keep in mind that these scores are highly subjective, certainly not scientific, and are intended only as a very general guide to help people seeking to work on self-improvement. Also remember that regardless of your position on the chart today, what matters is to do everything possible, in every minute of every day, to move closer to the upper-right corner of the upper-right quadrant where the highest possible levels of both technical competency and charisma are shown, thus increasing your chances for success in both your career and your life.

FOR REFLECTION AND DISCUSSION

When was the last time you actually worked with the product(s) you support?

How have you shown compassion toward others during the past week?

When do you find yourself most compassionate? How about least compassionate?

Think of someone to whom you simply can't relate. Try to be empathetic toward that person. What would it be like to be in her or his situation?

Think of someone for whom you have no respect. Maybe it's a co-worker or a relative. Now, think of things you can do the next time you're with that person to treat him or her with respect, as one human to another. How can you maintain your own self-respect in the process?

In anticipation of your next conversation with someone close to you, perhaps your spouse, your child, your sibling, or a close friend, how can you ensure you're really listening to what she or he is saying? What can you do to ensure you're really listening and not just going through the motions?

To-Dos

Set up a test lab where you can experiment with the product(s) you support.

Perform an act of kindness for another person that no one knows about but you. Make it someone you don't like.

Volunteer to help someone less fortunate than yourself, perhaps at a homeless shelter, food bank, or children's hospital.

Find someone who believes completely differently from you, perhaps on politics or religion. Ask that person to explain their feelings to you. Promise that you won't interrupt, argue, or pass judgment. Tell him or her that you're working on being a better listener and want to make sure you understand her or his point-of-view. Listen to what that person has to say, asking questions for clarification, and explain it back to his or her satisfaction. Look for common ground.

CHAPTER TWO:
PRACTICAL EMOTIONAL INTELLIGENCE

"Respect, tolerance and understanding for culture and religion are absolutely necessary in times of challenge and controversy. They are, in fact, the roots of character in times of great stress."

—Army Lt. Col. Christopher P. Hughes

Most of the people who work in IT are pretty bright. In fact, some of the most intelligent people in the world work in our field. Why is it, then, that some of us have a very difficult time keeping a job? I know someone who is much smarter than I am. In fact, he's a member of Mensa, but he has a hard time keeping positions at companies. I think the reason is because, although his IQ score is very high, his EQ (emotional-intelligence quotient) probably scores pretty low. You see, his IQ score gets him the job, but his inability to get along well with other people ultimately does him in. If you're not consistently getting the kind of responses you want from other people, maybe it's your EQ!

Emotional intelligence is a frequently used term in today's business circles. It refers to your ability to identify your own emotions and the emotions of others and respond appropriately.

In a nutshell, emotional intelligence boils down to the following four traits:

- The ability to recognize emotions in yourself and others

- The ability to respond appropriately to emotions

- The ability to control your own emotions

- The ability to influence a desired emotional response in others

Dr. John D. Mayer, a personality psychologist at the University of New Hampshire offers this definition: "Emotional intelligence represents an ability to validly reason with emotions and to use emotions to enhance thought." (Mayer 2005-2012)

Is the practice of emotional intelligence important and does it work? Consider the following story:

In April of 2003, Army Lt. Col. Christopher Hughes was leading a group of soldiers to meet with Ayatollah Sistani in the Iraqi city of An Najaf. They had been invited by the Ayatollah to discuss a fatwa, a religious proclamation, to help stop fighting in the city. As Hughes and his soldiers approached the mosque, an angry crowd of Iraqis confronted the patrol. Agitators had spread rumors that the soldiers were going to arrest the Ayatollah. As the crowd grew, becoming more agitated and aggressive, Col. Hughes initially thought to fire warning shots into the air, but he reconsidered and instead told his soldiers to "take a knee," point their weapons to the ground, and smile. The colonel recognized that the crowd didn't understand the patrol's intention and that he had to find a way to communicate to them that he and his soldiers were not a threat. Upon seeing the soldier's non-threatening stance and actions, the crowd's mood morphed from agitation to relief. Colonel Hughes then ordered the patrol to retreat and, as they retreated, he turned, faced the crowd, put his right-hand over his heart, and bowed, a gesture of respect that means "Allah be praised." The colonel could have taken a more traditional approach to conflict and fired a warning shot with his weapon, but by responding in an emotionally intelligent manner, he diffused an explosive situation. Not only were he and his soldiers able to retreat safely, they achieved a PR coup that undermined the agitators attempts to cast the Americans in a bad light. What's more, that night the Ayatollah issued a fatwa to the people of Najaf telling them not to interfere with the Americans entering the city. (Hughes 2007)

BONUS VIDEO: BUSINESS EMO:
EMOTIONAL INTELLIGENCE

Check out my video on emotional intelligence on my YouTube channel at *www.doncrawley.com/videos*.

EMOTIONAL MATURITY

The study of emotional intelligence actually goes back to Darwin's early work studying the importance of emotional expression for survival. In the early 1900s, researchers coined the term "social intelligence" to describe the skill of understanding and managing other people.

Someone who is emotionally intelligent is able to quickly recognize emotions in him or herself and deal appropriately with those emotions. He or she is able to manage emotions. Someone who is not emotionally intelligent, on the other hand, may not immediately recognize emotions and may let her or his emotions do the managing.

Consider this example: John is called into his boss's office and told his job is being eliminated. He wasn't expecting this news, so he is completely surprised. Upon hearing the news, he pauses for a moment and considers his options.

He chooses to remain calm, asks what his options are for severance and references, expresses his disappointment to his boss, shakes hands, and leaves. John is reacting in an emotionally intelligent manner.

Now, consider this example. Jared is called his boss's office and is told his job is being eliminated. He also wasn't expecting the news, so he, too, is completely surprised. He immediately starts swearing at his boss, accusing her of unfair treatment and incompetence, storms out of her office, and slams the door behind him. Jared is reacting in an emotionally stupid manner.

While most of us can understand Jared's reaction to the bad news, I think we can also agree that his reaction is self-destructive, especially in comparison to John's reaction.

The good news for most of us is that emotional intelligence skills can be learned and can improve over time. The general consensus is that traditional IQ doesn't change during a person's lifetime, but with practice, you can raise your EQ.

Emotional intelligence is both an academic pursuit and a practical or lifestyle pursuit. This chapter is concerned with the practical aspects of emotional intelligence. There is a body of thought that suggests emotional intelligence is more important as a measure of ability than intellect.

As mentioned earlier, from a practical standpoint, emotional intelligence involves four areas or abilities:

- The ability to recognize emotions in yourself and others

- The ability to respond appropriately to emotions

- The ability to control your own emotions

- The ability to influence a desired emotional response in others

For the purpose of this chapter, it may help you to think of emotional intelligence as emotional maturity.

Gradually, as we live and experience different people and situations, we develop methods of responding to those people and situations. Sometimes, we learn how to deal with people and situations by watching others, such as our parents, teachers, respected friends, celebrities, or leaders. Some of the people we watch demonstrate strong emotional maturity; others show immature behavior indicative of a lack of emotional intelligence. Other times, we read and study how to react to various people and situations. Often, our responses are shaped by a combination of external influences and things we read and study.

THE ABILITY TO RECOGNIZE AND RESPOND TO EMOTIONS IN YOURSELF AND OTHERS

The ability to recognize emotions in others through facial expressions, tone of voice, verbal cues, and body language is what allows you to move into the remaining abilities. Similarly, the ability to recognize emotions within yourself through feelings and physical responses also allows you to move into the remaining abilities.

Think about times when you've observed the expression on people's faces. Can you always tell what the people are thinking based on their expressions? Are you sure?

Sometimes, it's possible to tell how or what a person is feeling by his or her facial expressions. Facial expressions, however, can be deceiving. The same is true with body language. Many books and articles have been written about how to read eye movement, facial expression, and body language. Perhaps you've heard someone say that people who won't look you in the eye are being deceitful. Perhaps that's true with some, but consider Larry, who used to work for me. Larry would never look me in the eye. When we first starting working together, it really bothered me. I thought he was being dishonest or hiding something. As we worked together, I realized that he was (and is) scrupulously honest. He was a great employee, but for some reason, he was uncomfortable looking at another person eye to eye. Compare Larry to Willie. Willie was a friend who had read of the importance of looking people in the eye when talking with them. He wouldn't move his eyes off of you during conversation to the point where it became uncomfortable. Eventually, I had to look away. I never felt that Willie was dishonest, but I often wondered if he questioned the honesty of others since all of us would wither under his glare!

Certainly, there are cultural considerations, too. Some cultures, such as Muslim, Japanese, East Asian, and Nigerian, may influence an individual's eye contact or facial expression styles.

A STATE OF RAPPORT

Rapport is a relationship in which two or more people feel they're in sync with each other, in a state of harmony. That doesn't mean there's no' disagreement; it just means that the people in the relationship can work with each other toward a common objective. In the case of technical or customer support, it means that we, as support providers, are able to work with our customer or end user toward resolving a problem or implementing some sort of solution.

Psychologist and author Daniel Goleman believes that there are three ingredients of rapport (Goleman 2006):

1. Both people are paying attention; you're really attuned to each other.
2. The non-verbal communications, such as your gestures and body language, look like a choreographed dance.
3. It feels good.

The key for you, as a support person, starts with the first ingredient. You must pay careful attention to what your user is saying. In other parts of this book, we mention repeating back what the user says with phrases, such as:

- "Let me make sure I understand you correctly. Your printer is printing pages upside down. Is that correct?"

- "Just to be sure I understand, let me repeat this back to you. You're able to connect to internal sites with no problem, but when you try to hit the Internet, you get a 404 error. Is that correct?"

- "So, if I understand you correctly, the new copier won't collate pages. Do I understand the problem correctly?"

Repeating back the issue(s) does three things: (1) helps ensure that you really do understand the issue, (2) helps the user feel comfortable that you really do understand the issue, and (3) starts the process of establishing rapport with your user.

SOUNDTHINKING POINT:
Explain the Process

Sometimes, if it's a simple problem, it can sound silly or condescending to repeat back the problem, especially immediately after the end user or the customer has just stated it. In this type of situation, tell the other person what you're doing so they understand what's going on. You might say, "I know this probably seems obvious, but I've found that, even with a simple problem, it helps to repeat it back, just to ensure I'm not missing anything or misunderstanding what the problem is. So, the problem is your computer can't seem to generate PDFs. Is that it?"

Researchers have discovered that the areas of our brain responsible for calming us under stress work more effectively in the presence of an empathetic person. As a tech support person, you are that empathetic person. Your calm, empathetic behavior actually triggers changes in the other person's brain chemistry helping them become calmer, even under stress.

In an article for the Harvard Business Review titled "The Human Moment at Work," psychiatrist Edward M. Hallowell writes about how to make contact with other people at work. Hallowell suggests that in order to create a human moment in which you truly connect with your co-workers, two ingredients must exist:

- People's physical presence

- Their emotional and intellectual attention

In other words, to paraphrase Hallowell, turn off your tablet, close your laptop, end your daydream, pay full attention to the other person, and do it in person!

Of course, you may not be able to do it in person, but still lose any distractions and give the other person your full attention, just the same as if you were in person.

The Ability to Respond Appropriately to Emotions

Once you're able to recognize and identify emotions in others, you're ready to work on responding appropriately to those emotions.

As an IT support professional, what is the primary objective of each interaction with your user? The obvious answer is that our objective is to help the user by solving the problem and leaving him or her with a good feeling about us and our department. Remember from the introduction that our objective is to effect a positive outcome for the end user, our organization, and ourselves. Really, nothing else matters.

INTERACTIVE EXERCISE, PART 1:
Responding to Emotions

Think about how you have responded ineffectively in the past to these emotions in others. Pick two items from the following list and write a brief description of how you responded to them (one or two sentences):

- Anger
- Hostility
- Sadness
- Jealousy

- Excitement
- Pride
- Nervousness
- Skepticism

INTERACTIVE EXERCISE, PART 2:
Responding to Emotions

Now, thinking about the same incidents as in part one of the exercise, consider what made your past responses ineffective in dealing with those emotions in others. Write one or two sentences to describe a better way to deal with people who are showing those same emotions you selected above.

- Anger
- Hostility
- Sadness
- Jealousy

- Excitement
- Pride
- Nervousness
- Skepticism

Now, set a goal to modify your future behavior in similar situations to more closely match what you wrote in part two of this exercise. It's likely that you won't always be successful, especially at first. Don't worry when you sometimes fall back into old patterns of behavior. Just consider each relapse as a learning moment and strive to do better next time. The important thing is to ensure that your overall behavior is moving toward your goal.

THE ABILITY TO CONTROL YOUR OWN EMOTIONS

The term "emotional labor" was first defined by the sociologist Arlie Hochschild as the "management of feeling to create a publicly observable facial and bodily display." A good example of emotional labor occurs when a server in a restaurant smiles and expresses positive emotion toward diners. As an IT support professional, you engage in emotional labor when you are pleasant and upbeat with your users and customers. Sometimes, when we're not feeling up to par, it can be especially laborious! It's still important to "put on our game face."

Pleasant and Positive

It's easy to be pleasant and positive when you're already in a good mood or when you're dealing with a user who is also pleasant and upbeat. Your challenge comes, however, in being pleasant and positive when you don't feel well, when you're stressed because of personal or work issues, when you're hung over, or when your user is stressed, argumentative, or generally unpleasant. As an IT support professional or customer service rep, you must put on your game face even when you may feel really bad. You can do that by controlling your own emotions.

Successful Servers "Get-It"

Think about restaurant servers. Their income is dependent upon satisfied customers. They understand that their tips are often based on how they make the customer feel. If they complain about things in their life or in the restaurant, when they cast a shadow of dread, it casts a negative aura over the customer's experience and the tipping rate will likely go down. Not only will the tips go down, it's likely that the customers won't return to the restaurant. On the other hand, if they create a positive, uplifting experience for the customer, the tipping rate will most likely go up and the customers will come back again and again.

 SOUNDTHINKING POINT:
Keep it Positive

Always keep things positive and upbeat. The people in your life, including your users and customers, will appreciate it and your evaluations will reflect it!

THE ABILITY TO INFLUENCE A DESIRED EMOTIONAL RESPONSE IN OTHERS

Research has discovered what is now being called a "social brain." This social brain actually connects to other social brains. Without going into deep scientific detail, think about the times you've been around other people whose mere presence affected you in one way or another. When some people enter a room, they brighten it up. Others bring a cloud of despair. Have you ever been part of a group decision-making process when you felt you knew the outcome of the process just before it was announced? Your brain (your social brain) is actually picking up subtle clues from others in the group which tell it how they're thinking and feeling.

In the same way that we can detect the moods of others, we can also influence the moods of others. When we're in a calm state of mind, we can influence others to be in a calm state of mind. Conversely, when we're agitated, we can influence others to become agitated as well.

HOW TO CONTROL YOUR OWN EMOTIONS

Although there are many techniques that can be used to control your emotions and your responses to others' emotions, here is one short-term and long-term solution.

First, the short-term solution: When you encounter an emotionally charged situation, pause. Just stop for a moment. When I was a child, my parents told me when I was angry to count to ten before doing or saying anything. That was good advice. Another tool used with children, but also with benefits for adults, is to think of a stoplight. When you encounter an emotionally charged situation, visualize a stoplight:

- Red: Stop. Calm down. Think before you act.

- Yellow: Think of a range of things you can do.

- Green: Choose the best one.

When you move to green, evaluate the best option in terms of creating a positive outcome for your end user or customer, the organization, and yourself.

So, that was the short-term solution. The long-term solution is meditation.

Studies have shown that, after as little as eight weeks of meditation, physical changes take place within the brain that help you respond more calmly and appropriately to stressful situations. Author Matthieu Ricard, often described as the happiest man in the world, suggests that a regular practice of meditation "reduces anxiety, the tendency toward anger, and the risk of relapse for people who have previously undergone at least two episodes of serious depression." (Ricard 2010) Meditation doesn't require that you isolate yourself on a mountain top in Tibet. There are many forms of meditation, including one suggested by author Viktor Davich, where you sit quietly with your eyes closed and focus on your breathing for eight minutes a day (Davich 2004). Search the web for more information on the myriad forms of meditation.

If you feel that meditation is not for you, consider finding ways to focus your mental and emotional energy on something other than just your work. For example, I play music and find when I'm practicing the piano or the pipe organ that I "get in the zone." Long-distance runners and yoga practitioners have a similar experience. People I've known who have an active prayer life also seem to be calmer than many other people.

Find something that leads you to your bliss. It should be something non-competitive. Such things may not have the same level of impact as meditation, but perhaps they'll help you learn how to maintain your calm. The point is to find ways to generally calm yourself.

EXERCISE:
Emotional Intelligence

Below are some behavioral habits of emotional intelligence. As you read these, rate yourself on each behavioral habit. Look at each of the habits and rank yourself on a scale of one to five with five meaning you agree with the statement completely and one meaning you disagree completely. Then add your scores to get the total.

1. I can easily identify my feelings.

2. I am capable of regulating my emotions.

3. I stand up for myself and my beliefs in a respectful manner.

4. I tend not to be impulsive.

5. I have good social skills.

6. I can positively influence the emotions of other people.

7. I'm non-judgmental of other people and their feelings.

8. I don't try to manipulate or overpower other people.

9. I am empathetic. I can see things from someone else's perspective.

10. I am kind to other people, even people I don't particularly like.

11. I'm willing to challenge my most deeply held beliefs and make life course corrections when appropriate.

12. I avoid labeling other people.

13. I am happy.

14. I am optimistic.

Scoring:

56+: You have a high level of emotional maturity, self-awareness and self-control. You have a positive and uplifting effect on the people around you.

42 – 55: Your emotional maturity level is higher than average. You can improve it even more by concentrating on self-awareness and control. Work on improving your social skills and developing increased empathy for other people.

28 – 42: You are aware of what emotional maturity is. To grow in emotional maturity, work on self-awareness, kindness, and empathy toward others. Reflect on past responses to others and consider ways to improve your responses in the future.

27 or lower: Consider how your responses to others are affecting your life, both personally and professionally. Chances are that you're not getting the responses you desire, so spend some time in reflection, considering how you can modify your beliefs and/or behaviors to gain more respect and cooperation from the people around you. Evaluate your beliefs and behaviors as to their kindness and empathy toward others. Ask for feedback on how to modify behaviors with negative effects. Be prepared for some surprising responses and do not be defensive!

ONLINE EQ RESOURCES

- Free emotional intelligence test: *www.queendom.com*

- 8 Minute Meditation website: *www.8minutes.org*

- My YouTube channel: *www.doncrawley.com/videos*

- John D. Mayer's EI site: *www.unh.edu/emotional_intelligence*

FOR REFLECTION AND DISCUSSION

When have you let your emotions control your actions to your detriment?

When have you felt proud of your ability to maintain your composure during times of stress?

Are there times when it's appropriate to let your emotions dictate your actions?

Have you ever misjudged another person's emotional state? What went wrong? How did you misjudge them? How could you do it differently in the future?

TO-DOS

Think about the times when you've reacted poorly to emotions in others. Think about what you did that didn't work. On a piece of paper, write down how you want to react the next time you encounter a similar situation. Remember to evaluate your reactions based on effecting a positive outcome for you, your customer or end user, your colleagues, and your company.

Try Viktor Davich's idea of meditating for just eight minutes each day for fourteen days in a row. At the end of the two weeks, ask yourself how you feel at the end of the meditation session. How do you feel overall?

CHAPTER THREE:

WHAT TO DO WHEN
THE USER ISN'T RIGHT

"Clever men are impressed in their differences from their fellows. Wise men are conscious of their resemblance to them."

—R.H. Tawney

I saw a post on a friend's Facebook page complaining about how rude his customers were. His comment was that "the 'customer is always right thing' had gone too far." While there's no doubt that there are rude people in the world, if we're consistently encountering them, maybe it's not so much of matter of them being rude as it is a matter of us not handling them well. In this chapter, I'm going to share some ways you can manage demanding users and customers in a positive and productive way, even when you feel that they don't deserve your help.

We've all heard the saying, "The customer is always right." The problem is that they're not always right, and sometimes they're just downright rude or even abusive. Paradoxically, it's during the times when they're upset to the point of rudeness that we have a chance to turn the situation around. The real problem occurs when they're silently upset and say nothing to us. In retail businesses, only 4 percent of dissatisfied customers ever say anything. Most of the rest simply quit doing business with the store. A related statistic is that "68 percent of customers quit doing business with a company because of a perceived attitude of *indifference* toward the customer by the owner, manager, or some employee." (Le Boeuf 2000) If we work at an internal help desk, we may not be concerned with losing "customers" since our end users and customers are to some degree a captive audience. In reality, they are still our customers and when we lose their confidence, we may not hear about it, but others in our organization will! They will talk about us behind our back around the water cooler, at the coffee machine, to co-workers and their bosses, and anyone who will listen. What's the risk in that? I call it "death by water cooler." When we lose the confidence of our end users or customers and they start speaking poorly of us behind our backs, we run the risk of losing our jobs to other individuals or through out-sourcing.

Are You Creating Advocates or Detractors?

We can create advocates among our users and customers by delivering outstanding customer service. Advocates speak well of us when we're not around to speak up for ourselves. The opposite occurs when we create detractors by not providing outstanding customer service to our end users and customers. It's our choice, and the actions we choose define us.

EXERCISE:
Personal Experience Reflection

Our focus is on working with users and customers to create the best outcome possible for them and for you. To be a savvy customer service agent or IT support person, you need to combine your solid product or technical expertise with communication skills and other techniques to create a win-win solution for both yourself and your end users or customers. You can learn how to handle frustrated or angry users and customers, how to project a caring attitude, how to use effective tone of voice and body language, how to handle the stress of your job, and how to say no without alienating the end user or customer.

Think back to the Hero/Villain exercise in Chapter One. Take a minute to list characteristics of the good support call. Ask yourself these questions:

- What was happening?

- What did the support rep say and do?

- How were you feeling?

- What were you saying, doing?

If you're working with a group, share your observations with the rest of the group members. Next, think about the bad support situation. Ask yourself the same questions as above:

- What was happening?

- What was the support rep saying? Doing?

- How were you feeling?

- What were you saying, doing?

- What makes the difference between a successful support call and an unsuccessful one?

Again, if you're working on this in a group, share your observations with the group.

WHO ARE YOUR USERS
AND CUSTOMERS?

One of the biggest challenges you face as a customer service rep or an IT support person is dealing with users and customers who become angry and want to take their frustrations out on you. On top of a busy schedule, hard-to-solve technical problems, and pressure, you are sometimes faced with an unreasonable person, who despite your best efforts, ends up being angry not only at the situation but also at you.

The happiness of your users and customers is your concern because you are paid to help them solve their problems. In order to keep your job and enjoy what you are doing, you need to earn their respect. When they respect you, they pay attention to your advice. When they don't respect you, they ignore you or complain that you're not helpful.

Even if users and customers are wrong or demanding, you must learn how to treat them with respect, dignity, courtesy, and professionalism. You might think it sounds unfair that you have to work extra hard to appease them when they're wrong or out of control. But until users and customers know you care about them and their situation, they will not be able to appreciate your knowledge and problem-solving skills. If you want to be treated well, you need to seek to understand your users and customers, uncover their motivations, and connect with their desired outcome. As Martin Luther King, Jr. said, "People don't care how much you know until they know how much you care."

Are Your Conversations Cooperative? Follow These Four Maxims

When we're talking with an end user or a customer, we want to ensure our conversations are effective, that they make good use of our time and that of our customer or end user. One way to ensure that conversations are effective is to ensure they are cooperative, a process of give-and-take. Paul Grice was a professor at the University of California, Berkeley, and a philosopher of language who identified four maxims of conversation that describe the elements of successful cooperative conversation:

- **The Maxim of Quality**: Be truthful. Do not say something you believe to be false and do not say something for which you lack adequate evidence. ("I read it on Facebook, so it must be true.")

- **The Maxim of Quantity**: This maxim is about the quantity of information. Say as much as required for the purpose of the conversation, but nothing more.

- **The Maxim of Relation**: This maxim is about relevance. Keep your part of the conversation relevant to the rest of the conversation.

- **The Maxim of Manner**: This maxim is about being clear. Grice writes, "Avoid obscurity of expression. Avoid ambiguity. Be brief (avoid unnecessary *prolixity*). Be orderly." (Grice n.d.) (Don't feel bad, I had to look up *prolixity*, too. It strikes me that Grice's use of the word prolixity violates this maxim. Still, his point is well taken.)

If I were to summarize the Gricean Maxims, I would boil it down to this: In conversation, be respectful of the other person and be concise, don't waste their time or yours. Isn't that really what we want from other people who are speaking to us?

When we're talking with our end users or our customers, our conversations are better when we keep the four Gricean Maxims in mind. I've even noticed when I'm speaking with other people in general that the conversation is at its best when I'm following the these maxims (and I didn't even know about them until I started conducting research for this book).

DEALING WITH ANGER

What Is Your User or Customer Angry About?

It is sometimes said that anger is the only emotion that does not stand alone. What do you think this means? Anger usually results from or masks another emotion.

What are some other emotions that might result in an angry user?

A customer or user can become upset or seem angry for a number of reasons. You have no way of knowing what happened to the user or customer immediately before you encountered him or her. For example, she may have just received bad news about a close family member. He may have just received divorce papers. She may have just received a bad diagnosis from a doctor. Any number of other things could be affecting his or her emotions and behavior. Sometimes, even though the anger seems directed at you, it may, in fact, have nothing (or little) to do with you.

To be able to identify underlying emotions is to understand the other person better. This is a good skill to acquire and will improve your ability to diffuse someone's anger and move on to resolve his or her technical or product issue. Not only will the ability to understand users and customers improve your support work, this sensitivity will also be useful in all aspects of your life.

First Steps When Someone Is Angry

It is often necessary to appease the customer or user before you fix the problem. This may take several tools that you need to arm yourself with: Listening with empathy, apologizing when necessary (either out of sympathy or in response to some sort of failure), and headlining (telling what you are going to do before you do it) to create a satisfied user. Sensitivity to the user is important because it helps us deliver bad news in an acceptable way. It all goes back to empathy—walking a mile in the other person's shoes. Often, a successful support session involves negotiating an acceptable outcome. Negotiating with a customer or user is most successful when you use a win-win approach.

Your skill in handling their problem and the words you choose are the keys to keeping good relations with your users and customers and being able to work with them to their satisfaction. Angry users and customers present an opportunity to create loyal and supportive users and customers if you don't let them ruin your day. It starts with identifying what users and customers want from you, and then making sure that you are delivering what they want using your best skills.

Three Tips for Dealing with an Angry Person

Here are three things we can do to help manage the situation when we're dealing with anger in another person, such as a customer or end user:

1. **Pause and keep calm**. In my own experience, when I've encountered someone who was expressing anger to me, it seems like I've sometimes become competitive. Recognizing that, I'm getting better at pausing for a moment to gather my thoughts before reacting. Consider the wisdom of counting to ten before saying or doing anything. Maintaining your calm can help keep a situation from escalating. Breathe, try to step back from the situation (even if you can't step back physically, you can step back in your own mind).

2. **Don't try to use reason while they're angry.** Someone who is angry is under the control of their emotional brain. Reason and logic, while they're in an agitated state, will probably only make things worse. Save the reason and logic for later, after things have calmed down.

3. **Express empathy.** A sincere expression of empathy can be a powerful way to start calming things down. Use phrases like "I don't blame you" or "I'd probably feel the same way you do if I were in your shoes." You can even thank your customer or end user for bringing the problem to your attention!

Anger in another person can be intimidating or scary. It is, however, a fact of life that sometimes we have to deal with someone who's angry. When we can remember to pause, maintain our own calm, and show empathy toward the other person, we can start the process of de-escalating the situation and moving toward a positive outcome.

BONUS VIDEO: HOW TO DEAL WITH AN

ANGRY END USER

Watch my video on *How to Deal With an Angry End User* on my
video channel at *www.doncrawley.com/videos*.

When You Get Angry

A fact of being human is that we experience a wide range of emotions including happiness, pride, jealousy, sadness, and frustration. One emotion that can be difficult to deal with is our own anger. When our work involves serving others, we can sometimes encounter situations that make us angry. Anger, in itself, is not bad and, in fact, can serve as warning sign that something is wrong and be a positive catalyst for change. Anger, however, when it is expressed in hurtful or destructive ways can cause problems in relationships (both personal and professional) and lead to debilitating health problems. When not managed effectively, anger is a flame that consumes its host.

Here are three things we can do to help manage our anger when it comes up:

1. **Pause**. As with dealing with anger in others, pause. Count to ten before saying or doing anything. Think of the stoplight metaphor: Red means stop, yellow means consider your range of options, and green means choose the best one based on a positive outcome for yourself, any other people involved in the situation, and your organization.

2. **Be *assertive*, but not *aggressive***. Express yourself constructively and assertively, but not aggressively. Write it down, and don't mail it. The sole act of writing about how you feel is a way of taking action about whatever it is that's making you angry. It also allows you to reflect on the source of your anger later when you've calmed down. The difference between expressing your anger assertively and aggressively is this: When you express it assertively, you make clear what your needs and objections are. When you express it aggressively, you hurt other people. An assertive expression sticks to facts. An aggressive expression might involve name-calling and value judgments.

3. **Breathe**. Breathe deeply from your gut, not your chest. While you're breathing deeply, try repeating a calming word or phrase, such as "relax" or "be calm."

If you find yourself getting angry frequently, consider some long-term strategies to help with your anger. Such strategies might include yoga or meditation, an active prayer life, or anger management therapies. In some of my workshops and seminars, I offer participants a "get out of stress free" card.

On this card, you write things that give you a sense of peace or attach pictures of favorite people or places. When you feel yourself getting angry, you look at the card to help you calm yourself.

Remember, anger by itself is not bad and, in fact, can serve some very positive roles in our lives. It's when we express anger in hurtful or destructive ways that it becomes a problem. The great news about being human is that every one of us is capable of change. We can learn. We can grow. We can become the person we want to be.

BONUS VIDEO: THREE TIPS FOR ANGER MANAGEMENT

Watch my video on *Three Tips for Anger Management* on my video channel at *www.doncrawley.com/videos*.

HOW RESPONSIVE ARE YOU?

Responsiveness is the willingness to respond to end user or customer needs by answering their phone or email requests quickly, and being willing to do what it takes to respond effectively to a service request.

Responsiveness is adopting a can-do attitude and a willingness to go the extra mile for the customer. Multiple research studies support the theory that soft skills (such as listening, empathy, courtesy, and creating rapport) are more important than technical skills in the career advancement of any employee. This is especially true in the support industry, where most managers have realized that they must hire people who not only have an aptitude for technical knowledge but also have a good attitude or approach to serving customers, for the rest can be taught.

A positive attitude is the first step in building good soft skills. You have control over your attitude. Just like you can choose what clothes to wear in the morning, you can also choose what attitude to assume every day. Perhaps cliché, it's also true that you can choose to see the glass as half full, or half empty. Your approach, or attitude, toward life is a self-fulfilling prophecy. If your attitude is "Everyone has something to offer me, and every situation has something to teach me," then you will interpret everything that happens to you as an interesting journey. On the other hand, if you approach your job and your life in a less than positive way, every bump in the road will seem like a huge obstacle.

Who Is That in the Mirror?

At one point as a traveling trainer, I faced some of the typical challenges of life on the road. Things usually went very well for me, and on those rare occasions when things did "hiccup," they were usually minor. One particular week, however, I dealt with a major problem that had the potential to cause a major disruption in my business. As I looked back on what happened, I began to see the entire situation with new clarity. I made several mistakes.

- The first mistake was in making assumptions about what a vendor would do. I could have spent more time at their website and learned more about their policies and procedures. Instead, I spent a brief time skimming over their services and made assumptions about how to order a particular service and whether it was the right service for me.

- My second mistake was not contacting this vendor earlier to discuss how best to use their services (and whether they were even the right vendor for this job).

- The third mistake I made was trying to deal with this vendor while I was hurrying to catch a train. In other words, I was in a state of stress which undoubtedly came through in my voice (even though I don't think I was rude, demanding, or abusive).

As I dealt with this vendor in trying to resolve several problems, I received brusque (almost rude) customer service. I don't believe there is ever a reason to treat any customer in a manner that is anything other than cheerful, pleasant, respectful, and empathetic, but I wonder if there were subtle messages that I was sending that caused me to receive less than exemplary customer service. As I look back at my experiences with other people, I also need to look in the mirror. Am I doing everything I can to have a positive effect on everyone I meet? Have I gone out of my way to touch people in a positive way? When the world doesn't go my way, do I take a moment to stop and regroup, or do I complain to everyone around me so they can feel bad, too? I know I can't control other people, but I can certainly control how I appear when they look in my direction.

So, what are the lessons I learned, and how do they relate to you as a customer service rep or tech support pro?

Start Early

When you have plenty of time, you're more relaxed and things just seem to go better. Arrive at your desk early. Give yourself fifteen or twenty minutes before your shift starts to gather your thoughts and organize your workspace. Then later, when the day starts to get frantic, you'll find you're more in control of things. I knew a football coach who told his players, "If you're not fifteen minutes early, you're late."

We've all heard people say they were late because traffic was awful, the drawbridge was up, a train was blocking the road, or any of a multitude of other excuses. The truth is that when we're late, it's because we didn't leave early enough. No excuses.

Do Enough Research

As a tech support or customer service person, do you subscribe to news feeds and blogs about the products you support? Do you spend time each day reading articles and books related to the products you support? If you work in IT, have you set up a virtual lab using VMWare, VirtualPC, or VirtualBox so you can experiment and test your solutions before you offer them to your users? Do you personally use your company's products or services? Knowledge is power, and the more knowledge you have, the more you'll be empowered to delight your users with relevant, accurate solutions.

Focus

Focus on the task at hand instead of multitasking. This means, when your users or customers call needing help, you focus exclusively on them and nothing else. Even if you think you can multitask, don't let your callers know you're doing it while you're talking to them!

SOUNDTHINKING POINT:
The Myth of Multitasking

Many of us think we're pretty good at multitasking. The research disagrees. Stanford psychology professor Clifford Nass, in a 2013 interview on NPR, says we're fooling ourselves with our out-of-control multitasking: checking email, tweeting, texting, Facebooking, writing reports, watching television, and talking on the phone all at the same time wastes way more time than it saves. Not only that, but based on research done by Nass and other scientists, multitasking kills creativity and concentration as well. According to Nass, "The research is almost unanimous, which is very rare in social science, and it says that people who chronically multitask show an enormous range of deficits. They're basically terrible at all sorts of cognitive tasks, including multitasking." To hear the interview, search on the terms "nass myth of multitasking". If you really want to be creative and productive, focus on the task at hand and block out distractions.

Look in the Mirror

When the world is crashing around you, before you do anything else, look in the mirror. Maybe you can't control the rest of the world, but you are in complete control over how you view the world and what's happening in it.

As a desktop support professional, take a moment to ask yourself the following questions:

1. Do I put myself in the user's shoes?
2. Do I take ownership of a problem and see it through to completion?
3. Am I willing to help both users and co-workers?
4. Do I consciously assume a positive outlook with my users and co-workers?
5. Am I dignified, respectful, and courteous to the user?
6. Do I treat everyone with dignity, respect, and courtesy?
7. Do I speak and conduct myself confidently with users?

If you answered yes to at least five, you are on the right track to creating a positive position from which to serve your users for the best results. If you answered yes to fewer than five, your attitude might be keeping you from doing your best to create the proper environment for success in your job.

BONUS VIDEO: HOW TO MANAGE YOUR
DAY SUCCESSFULLY

Watch my video on *How to Manage Your Day Successfully* on my YouTube channel at *www.doncrawley.com/videos*.

WHAT USERS AND CUSTOMERS REALLY WANT

Take a minute to make a list of what you are looking for when you call for help or support on a product or service. What is important to you? Users and customers care about the same things you do when they contact you for assistance.

They want:

- Dependable and reliable service

- Responsiveness

- Competence

- Empathy

- Professionalism

Dependable and Reliable Service

Users and customers should get the same courteous, pleasant, and knowledgeable service every time they contact your department. This means providing accurate support with consistent service and reliable follow-through on your promises.

To accomplish this, consider adopting the tactic of under-promising so you can over-deliver. In other words, set expectations with your user at a reasonable level, but one at which you can consistently exceed their expectations. That means giving yourself and your co-workers a cushion when making promises to users and customers. For example, if you need to research a problem for a user, and you think you can call them back in two hours, discipline yourself to tell the user that you will get back to them in, for example, four hours. This helps account for unexpected emergencies that might come up, yet still permits you meet your user's expectations. Using this technique, your users and customers will be wowed, and you will reduce your personal stress.

Responsiveness

Responsiveness is the willingness to respond to user and customer needs by answering their phone or email requests quickly and being willing to do what it takes to respond effectively to a service request.

Responsiveness is adopting a can-do attitude and a willingness to go the extra mile for the user. As mentioned earlier in the chapter, recent industry trends indicate that soft skills (such as listening, empathy, courtesy and creating rapport) are as or more important than technical skills in the career advancement of any employee. Most managers in the support industry know this and hire or promote accordingly.

Competence

Competence means providing correct, knowledgeable service, performed with accuracy and confidence. Here are a couple of good techniques to use to demonstrate your competence.

Tell your customer or user what you are going to do before you do it. This technique is called headlining, in the sense that a newspaper article's headline tells you what you are going to read before you read it. As a customer or user, it is very frustrating to be dealing with a service provider who does not tell you what he or she is doing. When there is silence on the phone, the caller may become confused or concerned that he has been disconnected, and this certainly does not assure the caller of your competence. You know you have not done a good job of headlining if, after a period of silence, your caller says,

"Are you still there?" The caller does not feel cared for if she has to guess if you are still on the line.

Headlining is the mark of a professional support provider. It is easy and quick to do, and creates a high degree of user or customer satisfaction. Use headlining when you need to take a moment to look up some information in the database. You can say, "It will take me just a minute to look that up in the database." This gives the caller the assurance that you are working on her or his behalf.

If the problem is going to require more than just a few minutes, give your caller the option of getting a call back from you instead of being on hold or listening to you work for an extended period of time. (Make sure to call him/her back when you say you will!)

Another way of providing assurance to users and customers is to build their confidence in your ability to help them. This can be done with a solution statement delivered once you understand and have confirmed the caller's problem. A solution statement simply tells the user that you can help them solve the problem. You can say, "From what you have told me, I know how to solve the problem."

Examples of Competence Statements

- "This is going to take me a moment. I'm not ignoring you." About every twenty to thirty seconds, say something like "I'm still working on it," "I'm still here," or "I haven't forgotten you."

- "I dealt with something similar recently. I can take care of that for you."

Maintaining Technical and Product Competence

Of course, competence is more than just the words you choose; you must also maintain product or technical competence. Today's world evolves so quickly that maintaining technical or product competence can seem overwhelming at times. Here are four keys to maintaining your technical competence:

1. **Be curious.** Curious people are always exploring. When you're curious, life is more interesting, and you find new ways of doing things and things you didn't even know existed, and you maintain a childlike sense of wonder and awe.

2. **Read ... a lot.** The fact that you're reading this book speaks highly of you. It's not that you're reading this particular book (as much as your author wants to believe that); that you're reading anything about how to do your job better is what speaks so highly of you. There are thousands, perhaps millions, of blogs and forums on the Web dealing with the same technologies you support. Microsoft, Cisco, Redhat, and most other vendors provide extensive support documentation at their sites. Microsoft even has free hands-on labs and how-to guides. Get one of my Accidental Administrator® books or one of the O'Reilly Cookbooks for the technology you support and work through configurations that are most interesting to you.

3. **Build a sandbox.** I first heard of an IT "sandbox" when I was working with some individuals from Kimberly-Clark Corporation in a PKI training session. The IT "sandbox" is another name for a testing lab where you can experiment without worrying about system failure. Today, it's often not necessary to set up a physical lab with multiple physical computers. Instead, you can use tools like VMWare (*www.vmware.com*) or VirtualBox (*www.virtualbox.org*) to create a virtualized lab environment in which you can test and experiment to your heart's content without worrying

about affecting end users. Some virtualization products are available for free, others at very low cost. (I use VMWare Workstation.) Use Google to learn more about virtualization and the vendors who create virtualization products. Even if you don't work in IT, you can still set up a sandbox using the products you support to gain great familiarity with them.

4. **Get trained!** As a training provider to the IT world, you'd certainly expect me to make this recommendation, and it's important. Training, whether in a college classroom, seminar, workshop, or conference environment, exposes you to new ways of thinking and doing. Online training can be an excellent solution, but participating in-person in classes allows you to interact with the instructor and the other students. It's through such interaction that you discover new concepts and new solutions to old problems. I discovered when I returned to college that just being in an educational environment got me thinking in new and positive ways. Additionally, great teachers and trainers challenge you and help you step outside your comfort zone, which is how you effect positive change in your career and in your life.

Being great at your job isn't necessarily easy, but it's immensely rewarding in terms of personal satisfaction, career options, and financial rewards.

Empathy

Empathy means providing caring and personal service. Support personnel convey empathy when they listen for the hidden meaning in what a user is saying, acknowledge the emotion, and offer caring assistance.

Empathy is especially important when dealing with a user who is irritated, angry, or emotional. When we are emotional, it is difficult for us to act rationally. This is because of the way our brains are structured. The amygdala is a small portion of our brain that controls our fight-or-flight instinct. Sometimes known as the emotional brain, and a relatively primitive part of the human brain, it can in essence "hijack" the rest of our more rational, analytical brain and take control. In fact, the term "amygdala hijack" is sometimes used to describe what happens in such situations.

To get someone out of the grip of the emotional brain and pass the power over to the analytical brain takes one of three things:

1. Intervention of a skilled listener or support professional
2. Concerted effort on the part of the emotional person
3. Passing of time

It is important to understand this as we deal with emotional, upset, or angry users and customers. Empathy is a remedy for calming an emotional person by simply acknowledging the emotion that the user feels. Empathy is very powerful because it diffuses emotion. If you want to be able to deal rationally with an emotional user, or if you simply want to ensure that an interaction does not escalate into an emotional one, remember to use empathy. If sincerely applied, it works like a charm in most situations.

Examples of Empathy Statements

- "I can hear how frustrated you are."
- "I can see how that would annoy you."
- "That's terrible!"
- "I understand how time-critical this is."
- "I would be unhappy if that happened to me, too."
- "I'm sorry that happened to you."

Professionalism

Professionalism means that how you speak and act and the emails or other materials you send reflect a high level of training and expertise. This becomes the professional image that you project to your users and customers. Much of our support is provided via the telephone. Here are some ways you can project a professional image to users and customers on the phone (or, frankly, in other methods of communication, too):

Smile

A smile on your face affects how your voice sounds on the phone. Smiling creates more pleasant resonance in a phone voice and is the first step in conveying a professional image. Maybe you've heard the phrase, "Smile and dial!" Some professionals who use the phone place mirrors at their desks so they can check their smile before talking on the phone.

Approach Each Interaction with a Positive Attitude

We know how a positive attitude is self-fulfilling. Your users and customers deserve a cheerful approach on every interaction. IT support personnel must perform extreme self-care in order to approach each phone call positively. If you feel you cannot be positive on the next phone call, ask your manager for a few minutes to take a walk or get a bite to eat. Your users and customers will be grateful that you took a break so you can return with a fresh attitude.

Speak Clearly

Mumbling conveys a lack of confidence. Enunciating and speaking in a clear, moderate tone of voice conveys confidence and professionalism. Listen carefully to yourself speak, and you will be amazed how much better your enunciation becomes. You will also pay more attention to the words you use.

Develop Rapport

Recall from earlier in the book that being "in rapport" means being in sync with another person's communication style. Have you ever instantly liked someone you were talking to over the phone, even though you'd never met them before in your life? Chances are that you were in rapport with them. They may have been using some techniques that are very effective to make you feel at home with them.

Mirroring is a subtle way to conform your behavior to match the behavior of your user. It is the genuine search for areas of similarity between you and your communication partner, and its purpose is to make people feel comfortable with you. There are several auditory ways to create rapport through mirroring on the phone:

- Matching your rate of speech and the tone of your voice to that of the user

- Using the same verbal expressions and repeating or paraphrasing what the user has said

If the user is speaking slowly, and you normally speak very quickly, moderate your normal rate of speech. If your user is using a loud voice, speak up just a bit. Remember, you do not want to mirror the aggressive behavior or anger of a user. If the user uses an incorrect technical term, use the same language at first and then gently educate the user, saying for example, "We also call that the file extension."

Repeating or paraphrasing is an excellent way to mirror the user's communication style. It is also a powerful listening technique. A good time to use paraphrasing is when you are asking a series of questions while troubleshooting. You can repeat or paraphrase a few key words of the user's answer to confirm your understanding.

Avoid Slang, Colloquialisms, Profanity, and Terms of Endearment

People from other parts of the country or the world may not understand some of the terms you may use when speaking casually to your friends. Customer support personnel should always use professional language in speaking to users and customers. Professional language does not include profanity, terms of endearment, or slang nicknames like dude, bud, honey, sweetie, buddy, or pal, or other forms of slang. An exception to this rule is when speaking with a user with whom you have a personal relationship, but a wise support person will still exercise caution when communicating with any user.

Avoid Overly Familiar and Condescending Nicknames

Never refer to your user with overly familiar or condescending nicknames, such as Dude, Bud, Honey, Sweetie, Buddy, Pal, Son, Young man, Young lady, Old man, Old lady, Kid, Sugar, or similar names. Sir or Ma'am are usually appropriate.

SEQUENCE FOR HANDLING USER CALLS

Here is a sequence to a support interaction that you can use to make sure your calls and written communications go the way you want them to. Following these steps will ensure that you give the best customer service as you resolve user issues. It will also help you to diffuse users and customers who are angry or upset.

1. The Greeting
2. Active Listening
3. Gain Agreement
4. Apologize/Empathize/Reassure
5. Problem Solve
6. Confirm Resolution

The Greeting

Start off your phone call with a greeting that is sincere yet inviting. Your greeting, the first time your caller hears your voice, sets the tone for the rest of the conversation. The first impression is the one that lasts. You want to be inviting and sound interested in what the caller has to say. If you approach each call with a genuine desire to help, your sincerity will come through in the tone and quality of your voice, and your words will be heard and appreciated. You will be setting the stage for a good outcome.

Be careful about using a lengthy, canned greeting like "Gigantacorp Computer Services Help Desk, where we always strive for top-rated service. This is Tom Helpful, MCDST, CCNA. How may I provide you with excellent service this fine morning?" Something more appropriate is, "Computer Services Help Desk. This is Tom. May I help you?"

Just in Case You Get Disconnected

Shortly after your initial greeting, be sure to get a call-back number for your user in case the call gets disconnected.

Active Listening

When you actively listen, you are demonstrating to your user that you hear what they are saying and you are taking in the important information they are providing you about their issue. Use verbal cues, such as "all right," "OK," "I see," and "I understand." You will also need to deliver them with empathy and understanding in your voice. This is also the phase where you gather information such as the software version that's installed and similar information to ensure you provide the correct solution.

Gain Agreement

Gaining agreement with the user on why they are contacting you is an important part of the overall user support process. Gaining agreement is paraphrasing or reflecting back what you believe to be the user's problem. Taking time to gain agreement gives you an opportunity to check your understanding of the situation so that you address the correct issue to your user's satisfaction.

Examples of Gaining Agreement With the User

"So you are trying to create a PDF and the graphics don't look right. Is this the main issue you are calling about today?"

"So what we need to focus on today is finding out why your new laptop battery charge is so weak. Is that correct?"

Sometimes, it might be necessary to say things like, "I'd like to just quickly go through a check list to make sure I completely understand the issue. Some of the things may seem obvious, but I want to make sure I don't overlook anything. Is it OK to go through the checklist with you?"

Once you have gained agreement, your user may still be a little frustrated, but feeling more comfortable because of the professionalism and empathy you have displayed so far.

Show Empathy and Reassure

After you gain agreement, it is important to let the user know that the frustration or disappointment they are experiencing is justified and understandable. For example, "I think anyone in your situation would be frustrated" or "I can understand why you are disappointed at this time." Acknowledging feelings helps the user know that they are justified in their frustration.

Reassurance fosters confidence and trust by assuring the user that you will do whatever you can to help. Reassure the user that you will do your best to resolve their issue as quickly as possible.

An Example of How to Show Empathy and Reassure

"OK, so I understand the situation to be that you finally convinced
your boss to get you a new laptop because you needed a more
reliable machine for all the travel you have been doing lately. You
got the new laptop, and now the battery won't hold a charge. I think
anyone in your situation would be very dissatisfied at this point. Let
me assure you, you have reached the right place! Let me see what
I can do to help."

In the preceding example, the exact words are probably different from the
words that you would choose. The point is not the verbiage but the underlying
message, which includes agreement on the problem, empathy, and reassurance.

At this point, your user will likely be much more flexible and willing to seek
resolution through troubleshooting than they were when they first contacted
you. By this time, the user is probably going to thank you. They realize at this
moment that they are with a competent, caring, intelligent technical support
person who is actually going to help them resolve the situation. The next step
would be to consider whether an apology is in order.

Apologize If Needed

Apologize, if necessary. Sometimes, the user appreciates an apology for the less
than satisfactory situation they are in, regardless of who is at fault. It's human
nature. You should apologize when:

- You have made a mistake.

- Someone else has made a mistake.

- The failure of a product or service frustrates the user.

An example of an appropriate apology is: "I am sorry that your laptop battery is defective."

Avoid Automatic Apologies

Have you ever called customer service or technical support and had the support person apologize over and over again, even though the problem wasn't their fault or their company's fault? Such automatic apologies lack sincerity and authenticity. People can tell the difference and such apologies can undermine the credibility of a sincere apology later on. Always be authentic!

Problem Solve

Remember how, when you call for help with an order or support with a product, you want to talk to someone who takes a genuine interest in you and your situation. You want results. When you take on the user's problem or situation and work it as if it were your own, you will be providing outstanding customer service. Everything about your interaction with the caller will be genuine and positive. You will be creative when needed, taking into account exactly what the user has told you and trying your best to work toward a solution. Being a problem solver means that you treat someone the way you like to be treated, using all of your knowledge and skills to improve the caller's situation or dilemma. You go the extra step to research and implement the best solution. No matter what you are able to do for them, your users and customers will feel that they have been treated well, and will trust you and pay attention to the advice you give them. When you approach each interaction by giving it your full attention, you will receive positive feedback and be appreciated for your work—even when you can't do exactly what the user asks you to do.

Confirm Resolution

Before you disconnect from the user (regardless of how you're handling the support case, whether in-person, on the phone, in chat, or any other method), be sure you've resolved their problem. Here are some examples of questions you can ask to ensure you've actually resolved the case:

- "Does that take care of the reason for your call?"

- "Is everything OK now?"

- "Is it working satisfactorily now?"

- "Is there anything else I can do for you?"

The main thing is to put yourself in the user's position. Wouldn't you want your support rep to ensure your problem was adequately resolved before disconnecting?

Order Matters!

Isn't it interesting how the problem-solving process is one of the last steps? The steps leading up to problem-solving ensure that you understand what the problem is and that the user is confident of your ability to solve his or her problem.

BONUS VIDEO: **THE SIX STEPS IN**

A SUCCESSFUL SUPPORT CALL

Watch my video on *The Six Steps in a Successful Support Call* on my YouTube channel at *www.doncrawley.com/videos*.

INTERACTIVE EXERCISE:

Role Play with an Upset User

Work with a partner on this exercise. Think of a real-life customer service problem you can role-play. You should be the support person and your partner the end user seeking assistance.

Sample Scenarios

- "My taskbar keeps disappearing."

- "Why is my computer so slow?"

- "I was working on a large report for my boss. I'm sure I saved the file, but I can't find it anywhere."

You should come up with enough detail to talk for about three minutes. You may want to jot down notes or create a practice script. (If you choose to use a practice script, it should only be for the purpose of practicing. In the real world, be authentic and avoid reading from a script.)

Use your best communication skills to diffuse the situation, keep the call on track, and resolve the issue for user satisfaction.

Begin the role-play. When the call has ended, have your partner give you feedback on how you did using the techniques we just learned, including the sequence for handling user calls. Use the questions on the following page. Remember to be open to criticism. Don't get defensive or you won't gain anything from the exercise.

Evaluate the Role Play

1. Did you follow the sequence for handling a user call? Describe how you used each of the six steps.

2. Did your user feel good about what you said and how you reacted to their problem? Get their feedback on how you came across.

3. How did you demonstrate that you were listening?

4. Did your tone of voice reflect sincere empathy? How do you know? Did you use mirroring?

5. Did you acknowledge your user's feelings? What was their response or reaction?

6. How were you reassuring?

7. What did you learn from this experience?

RESPECT YOUR USERS' AND CUSTOMERS' TIME

Sometimes, problem solving takes longer than we expect. Even if your company or department doesn't have a time limit on calls, consider placing a limit on yourself. For example, suppose that a call or support visit is taking longer than you expect, when it exceeds the limit, say something to the customer or user like this, "This issue is taking longer than I expected. I want to respect your time, so how about if I continue working on it and communicate with you via email as I'm working on it? Of course, you're welcome to stay on the line with me. I just want to make sure I'm not taking too much of your time."

I listened to a recording of a support call where the issue couldn't be resolved right away. The caller was a nurse in a busy doctor's office. She was animated and friendly when the call began, but after eighteen minutes on the phone, her voice showed that she was frustrated and disappointed. To make matters worse, at the end of the call the support rep said, "Have a nice day." I realize, of course, that he said that out of habit, but it showed insensitivity to the caller and may have made the situation even worse. He should have let her get off the phone after five or six minutes, apologized that he wasn't able to resolve it, and promised to continue working to resolve it. He definitely should not have told her to have a nice day.

SOUNDTHINKING POINT:
Put a Time Limit on First Calls

Does your department have a policy on how long to keep a caller online during the initial call? If not, consider establishing your own personal policy. Establish a reasonable limit, perhaps five or six minutes, and, if you can't resolve the problem within that amount of time, explain to the caller that their issue is taking longer than you expected and offer to call them back. If it's necessary for the caller to participate in the troubleshooting process, ask if they'd prefer to do this at another time or if the present time is okay.

FOR REFLECTION AND DISCUSSION

Recall the last time you called a company, got disconnected, and had to go through the call tree and queue all over again. How did that make you feel?

Think back to a time when you were trying to get support for something and the support agent didn't find out which version of the product you were using. You ended up getting support for the wrong version and wasted your time with a solution that wouldn't work.

Have you ever had a support agent end a support session without confirming resolution? What did you have to do to get the issue resolved?

TO-DOS

Do a role-play with a colleague and work through each of the six steps. Practice until it becomes second nature.

Set up a test lab using a tool, such as Hyper-V, VMWare or VirtualBox. Install the software you support and experiment with some of the same scenarios your users might encounter.

If you don't work in IT, ask your boss if you can have access to some sample products to better familiarize yourself with them. See if you can re-create some of the more common problems customers call about.

Set your alarm for fifteen minutes earlier than usual and start leaving fifteen minutes earlier than usual to allow time for bad traffic, crowded trains or busses, or a raised drawbridge. Get the frantic out of your life! It's amazing how, when we're early, things are so much more calm.

Take an online class or watch a series of training videos. You'll find a wealth of free videos online by simply searching for whatever topic interests you. Set up your lab, find videos to watch, and follow along in your lab.

Take a class at the local community college.

CHAPTER FOUR

THE ART OF LISTENING WELL

"Most people do not listen with the intent to understand;
they listen with the intent to reply."

—Stephen R. Covey

O ne of the great paradoxes of life is that if you want to be known as a great conversationalist, don't talk but be a great listener. In this chapter, you'll learn the five levels of listening, the critical difference between the top level of listening and the lower four, and ten tips for being a good listener. Huh? Beg your pardon? What'd you say?

THE FIVE LEVELS OF LISTENING

We listen at five different and distinct levels. How you listen to your users and customers will have a significant impact on your success, that of your team, and that of the entire organization. As important as how you actually listen is how you are *perceived* to listen.

Ignoring

The lowest level of listening is called ignoring—not listening at all. If you are distracted by anything while talking to users or customers, they can get the impression that you are ignoring them, like interjecting while they are describing a problem, starting a conversation with another support rep during your support session, texting or Facebooking on your phone, or typing something into your computer while staring straight into the monitor. These types of things tell the other person you're not engaged with him or her.

Pretend Listening

Pretend listening is most easily explained in the face-to-face conversation. You're talking to the other person and they have that far-away, "backpacking in Brazil" look in their eyes. On the phone it happens when you say things like "I see," "Uh huh," and "OK" while working on an unrelated email, checking a social network, or playing a computer game. People can tell you're distracted.

Selective Listening

During selective listening, we pay attention to the person speaking as long as they are talking about things we like or agree with. If the speaker moves on to other things, we slip down to pretend listening or ignore her or him altogether.

Attentive Listening

Attentive listening occurs when we carefully listen to the other person, but while they're speaking, we are deciding whether we agree or disagree, determining whether they are right or wrong, and thinking of what we're going to say in response.

At all four of these levels, it should be evident that we are listening to our own perspective and, in most cases, with the intent to respond from our experience. We're less interested in gaining a complete understanding of what the other person is saying than in determining what we're going to say at the next break in the conversation.

Empathetic Listening

To be successful in providing support to end users and customers, you must teach yourself to treat every call as though it's the first time you've ever heard the problem, even though you may have heard it many times before. Discipline yourself to see it through the eyes of the customer or user. This is called empathetic listening. Empathetic listening is the highest level of listening and the hardest to accomplish.

Where Is Your Focus?

As you think about the five levels of listening, realize that the first four levels are self-focused, while the fifth level (empathetic listening) is focused on the other person. When your focus is completely on the other person and not on yourself, your level of service will be much higher.

HOW TO ACHIEVE EMPATHETIC LISTENING

What's Your Hurry? Be Patient

Users and customers who are rushed will be annoyed, not satisfied. They will feel that they did not get top notch service, and they'll feel let down. Slow down. Assess your customer's or user's urgency. What is their availability? What is their timeframe? What is their mood?

A customer or user may not be able to fully articulate the problem, and may stumble over an explanation, or take a long-winded approach to explaining what is wrong. Allow him or her to have time to finish the explanation. An issue that she or he mentions casually may be important. Your user or customer will appreciate that you took the extra time to listen and get involved, going the extra step to be helpful.

It's easy to place blame on the technology, the tools, other departments, a service provider, the management, the company or organization, or the user.

Be a problem solver, not a blamer. There's a fine line between accurately describing a problem and complaining about the company that sells the product or service in question. Most people want to know what the problem is, but they don't really care to hear our opinions about Microsoft, Apple, Ford, GM, or any other company.

Talk Less and Listen More

> *"Courage is what it takes to stand up and speak;*
> *courage is also what it takes to sit down and listen."*
>
> —Winston Churchill

Users and customers are very important people. They are the reason we have jobs. They deserve our undivided attention and our most gracious approach to problem-solving. We may know more than they do on the reason for their call, but we will only be successful when our user or customer is satisfied with the outcome of the call or visit.

Listen carefully to everything your caller says, as if there is going to be a test at the end of the conversation. Empathize with her problems and issues. Jot down notes and ideas to respond to, without losing your attention. Make comments to acknowledge his problem and position. Repeat the points your caller made in your own words (paraphrase) to make sure you understand and to let her know she has been heard.

Be careful not to use technical jargon and acronyms your users or customers don't understand. You risk confusing, intimidating, or angering them. By empathetically listening, you will be able to detect a person's level of expertise. You can also politely ask her how technical she would like you to be. In the same way that a less technically oriented user could get intimidated or angry by overly technical explanations, a more technically oriented user could get frustrated or angry by overly simple explanations (or a condescending attitude on your part). Be sensitive to the person to whom you're speaking. Regardless of his level of technical competence, make sure you have given him permission to interrupt you and ask for an explanation or clarification if he is confused by your explanation.

At the end of the call, do a short recap of what you have discussed, what approach you are suggesting, and any follow-up on your part or the customer's or user's part that is needed. Be specific about how you will follow up, what you will do, and what he or she can expect and when it will happen.

Create a Human Moment

Remember Hallowell's "Human Moment" from earlier in the book?

Put down the iPad and cell phone, turn off the computer, close the book, abandon the daydream, and focus entirely on the other person!

TEN KEYS TO BEING A GOOD LISTENER

1. Stop talking.
2. Lose distractions, including internal distractions from your mental clutter of things like to-do lists and plans for the weekend, as well as external distractions, such as cell phones, computers, and open books.
3. Focus on what the other person is saying as though there will be a test at the end of the conversation.
4. Keep your mind open to the possibility of new information. Try not to let your personal beliefs close your mind to new ideas.
5. Use physical and verbal responses, appropriately timed, to show you're listening, such as nodding your head, raising your eyebrows, saying "uh huh" and "oh."

6. Let the other person finish what he or she is saying. Resist the temptation to jump in with your response.

7. Ask questions for clarification as needed, but only after letting the other person finish.

8. Repeat back what the other person said. You can say things like, "I want to be sure I understand you, so please let me repeat back what you just said." Then repeat back what you think was said and say, "Is that correct? Is that the message you wanted to convey?"

9. Silence or a pause in the conversation does not necessarily mean you have to jump in and speak right away. Sometimes, you're better off allowing silence while you process what you've just heard.

10. Be sensitive to the non-verbal cues.

BONUS VIDEO: 10 WAYS TO BE

A BETTER LISTENER

Watch my video on *10 Ways to Be a Better Listener*
on my video channel at *www.doncrawley.com/videos*.

For Reflection and Discussion

Have you ever been talking with someone while he or she is texting or Facebooking? How did that make you feel?

How would you listen differently to a person if you wanted to understand her or him instead of just mentally preparing a response?

Has anyone ever finished sentences for you and completely changed the meaning of what you intended to say? How did that make you feel?

To-Dos

Find a friend you respect but who feels differently from you on an important issue. Ask him or her to explain how they feel and promise that you won't interrupt or challenge what's being said until your friend is convinced that you completely understand how she or he feels. Ask questions for clarification, but do not let your feelings influence the conversation.

Ask your spouse, partner, significant-other, or close friend how his or her day was. Ask questions to gain a deeper understanding and avoid talking about your day. (Caution: For some people, they'll be suspicious and wonder about your ulterior motives!)

The next time someone tries to talk with you, stop what you're doing. Close your laptop or turn off your tablet, face the other person, and focus completely on what she or he is saying. If you really need to finish what you're doing, say so and say you want to give the other person your full attention as soon as you're done.

MAKING SURE THEY KNOW YOU CARE

"Positive thoughts yield positive language yield positive results."

—Paul R. Senness

In working with end users, customers, and technical support staff, the most common phrases I hear relate to how much a support person cares. Similar to the four traits of the customer service masters, the simple act of caring about your fellow human being is the starting point for providing great customer service. If you truly care about your fellow humans, the rest of the customer service skills just fall in place naturally.

MAKING SURE THEY KNOW YOU CARE

Remember the previously quoted study that 68 percent of customers are lost due to perceived indifference? In a busy IT department, we sometimes forget that providing excellent service involves more than just fixing the problem. Outstanding service includes making users and customers feel good about their interaction with us by quickly creating a human bond.

Please understand that when I suggest we create a human bond with our customers or users, I'm not suggesting that we should attempt to create a deep and personal friendship. What I'm suggesting is something more along the lines of what happens when one person performs a simple act of kindness for another. Most of the time, such an act does not lead to a lasting friendship, but it does create a good feeling between the two people. Additionally, it can have a ripple effect as both people share their good feeling with others.

THE THREE COMPONENTS OF COMMUNICATION

- Words

- Tone of voice

- Non-verbal cues

When you can hear and see the person you are talking to, your message is comprised of words, tone of voice, and non-verbal cues, also known as body language. An often quoted research study by Albert Mehrabian (currently Professor Emeritus of Psychology, UCLA) suggests, when conveying feelings or attitudes, that words carry 7 percent of the message impact and tone of voice carries 38 percent. That means body language conveys 55 percent of the message impact. (The study has come to be known as the 7-38-55 percent rule.) Although the study dealt with communicating feelings and attitudes, the fundamental concept of body language as an important element of communication can also be applied to other forms of communication. The point is that body language plays a large role in how messages are communicated. Another point of the study is that your non-verbals need to be consistent with your verbal communication in order for you to have credibility with your listener. Imagine the confusion that might exist if you say to someone, "I'm really interested in hearing what you have to say," while you're typing text messages on your phone. There's a huge disconnect between the message communicated by the words coming out of your mouth and the message communicated by your actions.

> *What you do speaks so loudly that I cannot hear what you say.*
>
> —Ralph Waldo Emerson

Body language even influences communication during a telephone call. We all imagine what the other person is doing and looks like, and our choice of words, tone of voice, and professionalism (or lack thereof) heavily influences what the other person imagines us to be doing. It is incumbent upon us, as support professionals, to create an atmosphere that convinces the customer or user that you are sitting beside him or her as a teammate. Here are some golden rules to follow to create a satisfying experience for yourself and your customer or user:

- Use humor carefully (if at all)

- Never pretend you know what you are doing

- The power of positive

- Help the customer or user find a workaround

- Partner with your user or customer

- Be a valuable resource

- Teamwork

- Do one more thing

Use Humor Carefully (If at All)

Caution: Humor can offend when you don't expect it. Avoid topics like sex, race, religion, politics, or anything in poor taste. Remember, your job is to provide support, not to be a comedian.

Most people prefer dealing with people who enjoy themselves. Display a cheerful sense of humor coupled with good judgment and common sense. Laughing at yourself is usually safe, but unless you know the individual with whom you are working, tread lightly on other forms of humor.

A few users and customers will want to just take care of business. They're looking for customer service that is quick, efficient, and gets down to business, delivered by a person with a good attitude. Always respect your users or customers time; when they're in a hurry, just deliver the service with pleasant professionalism!

Of course, we're human, and it's difficult to avoid using your own support desk humor with your co-workers and friends. Some of your work stories can be very entertaining when used in the right circumstances. IT support desk humor is born from the tension between knowledgeable "power users" like ourselves and the users and customers who call us. Avoid, however, sharing such humor with end users and customers. Something you consider funny might have actually happened to the person who calls in and she or he might have found it embarrassing. If you bring it up in an attempt to be funny, you could cause that person to relive an embarrassing moment.

CHAPTER FIVE:
MAKING SURE THEY KNOW YOU CARE

What Is Funny to Some May Be Painful to Another

I don't normally teach end-user classes, but a client had an
emergency situation and needed someone to teach a basic Excel
class. They asked me to do it, and since they were an excellent
client, I agreed. During the class, I made a joke about someone
being confused by asterisks being displayed in a password field
instead of the actual password. Most of the people laughed,
but at the break one individual came up to me nearly in tears.
She explained that she had been confused by the asterisks
and felt that everyone was laughing at her. You might think she
was overreacting, but it doesn't really matter whether she was
or wasn't. What matters is that my actions unintentionally (and
unnecessarily) caused another human being pain. Since that time,
I've tried to be more sensitive to how my choice of words and
humor might affect another person. If I were a comedian whose job
is to make people laugh, I might feel differently, but I'm a teacher,
and my job is to educate. I need to be very careful of anything that
gets in the way of doing my job. Similarly, our jobs as support staff
are to support end users and customers and help them work more
effectively, creatively, and productively. We need to be very careful
of anything that gets in the way of doing our jobs.

Always be respectful of your users and customers, even when you don't think
they can hear what you say. Things said about someone have a way of getting
back to that individual. One of my most embarrassing moments occurred when
I said something negative about a person who was just around the corner and
heard every word.

Always assume that everyone can hear everything you're saying.

Never Pretend You Know What You Are Doing

Users and customers call in assuming we will instantly have the right answer. Recognize that no one is a fully qualified expert and that we all have a lot to learn.

Know your limits. You may not have all the answers, but you do have a set of customer service tools. Using all of the support tools will make you look competent and confident.

Dr. Stephen R. Covey, author of *The 7 Habits of Highly Effective People*, says that we all have a personality ethic and a character ethic. The personality ethic is what people see on the surface, much like what's above the water line of an iceberg. The character ethic lies deep beneath. If your personality is not buoyed up by strong character, you can come off as a phony. Perhaps not at first, but eventually your end user or customer will perceive the truth. The success and reputation of your department or company rests on the user's experience. If this trust gets broken through a "know it all" attitude, it will be a long road back to credibility. It is one thing to speak with a tone of authority and confidence, but something entirely different to come off as a "know-it-all." Remember, you will gain far more respect from your users and customers with a "Let me research that and get back to you" correct answer than with an expedient incorrect answer that may cause damage to the user's work and will certainly damage the company's or IT support center's reputation.

Sometimes, you can't fulfill what the user or customer is asking for. Instead of saying "no," focus on what you can do. Use "I can, will, do, yes, you bet, absolutely." There are a couple of ways we can do this. Users and customers don't expect us to be perfect. They do expect us to be honest. When we make a mistake, we must acknowledge it, apologize for it, fix it, and move on.

The Power of Positive

There are two self-fulfilling prophecies. One is "positive thoughts yield positive language yield positive results." It means that when we think about things in a positive way (our job, our abilities, our users and customers, and other aspects of our life), we tend to talk about those things in positive manner. A result of this is that we attract more positive results. The opposite end of the spectrum is also true—"negative thoughts yield negative language yield negative results." Think about these two approaches to life and the impact they have had on your experiences. Which approach puts you at ease and which puts you on edge? Which approach left you satisfied and which led to unhappiness? We are in control of and can choose our attitude. That choice significantly impacts not only our mood and outlook, but also that of everyone around us and those with whom we come in contact.

Of course, this doesn't mean every day will be nothing but fun. There will be difficult and frustrating days and events. That's part of life. The decisions we make in how to approach such challenges will determine the outcome and future for both us and our users or customers.

Here are some tips to create the positive climate we all like to respond to:

Help the Customer or User Find a Workaround

Sometimes, you have to be a creative solution provider.

- No email? Try a co-worker's computer, a smart phone or tablet, use Webmail, a personal account as a temporary solution while your office email account is being fixed.

- Is your shuttle not operating? Can you offer a voucher for taxi cab fare?

- Can't print? Ask a co-worker? Email the document to yourself and use Webmail at a different computer to retrieve and print the document.

- No shared access to something? Can you get in and email it to the people who need it?

- Does a client want a service you don't provide? Bite the bullet and call a competitor to meet the client's needs.

- Is a failed router or firewall preventing Internet access? Is there a coffee shop nearby? What about an Internet-enabled phone or tablet?

- Is a particular part out of stock? Perhaps you have a used part to offer as a temporary fix until the new part arrives.

Working With Workarounds

How did you feel when you crafted a successful workaround? Reflect on the following questions. If you're working in a group, share what you have done on the job to help users and customers when regular solutions failed.

How did this make you feel?

How did your user react?

What kinds of workarounds have you found for yourself in the past?

Partner with Your User or Customer

Become co-owner of the problem. Use "we" statements instead of "you." Let your user vent when necessary. Even if the user says "don't bother," do it anyway, and follow up with her. She will appreciate it.

Be a Valuable Resource

Instead of being the one who knows all and can fix anything, be the one who will find the best answer, see the problem through to a solution, and focus on what users and customers can do for themselves. Help them to get it done so they will feel good about the interaction. Most of us like to be self-sufficient. Anytime you can teach your users and customers to be self-sufficient, they will increase their skills, cut down on the need to call you again, and feel empowered. By empowering your users and customers, you are creating user satisfaction and a positive outcome.

One word of caution, times of high stress are not good times to teach a user or customer. In a high-stress setting, simply perform the repair or otherwise solve the problem. You can always go back later, when things have calmed down, to do the teaching.

Teamwork

Share ideas and solutions with your co-workers. You may be able to share knowledge or tidbits with them and they may be able to help you learn something you don't know. Set up a wiki for developing documentation and sharing knowledge. There are a variety of wiki software applications available, some open-source and some proprietary. Wikipedia runs on MediaWiki which is open-source software, available at *www.mediawiki.org*.

Do One More Thing

Whenever you feel that the user has reached a point where she or he is satisfied, do one more thing. It doesn't have to be anything big. Just a little something extra you can do for them or assistance you can provide makes all the difference.

A baker's dozen is thirteen, or one more than a conventional dozen. There are several theories about where the concept originated. Perhaps it's so the baker can taste his or her creation to make sure the other twelve are okay or maybe it's to give the customer something extra. What really matters is the idea of giving your customers or users more than they expect.

A Loving Approach to Ceramics

Kristin Love is a successful ceramic artist. She creates her own unique pieces of pottery and sells them through various channels including the Internet (*http://www.loveartworks.net*). Kristin believes in the "baker's dozen" concept. When you buy an item from her, she always includes a little something extra. The bonus items are not large or expensive, but their perceived value as a token of appreciation is huge. Imagine the customers delight at receiving a special surprise with their order!

How do you provide a "baker's dozen" to your users and customers?

Many support staff members are not in a position to include an extra item in the shipping box, but we can still find ways of providing extra touches for our users and customers. Here are some ideas:

- At the end of a support session, share a new keyboard shortcut you've just discovered (Be sensitive to their schedules. If they're obviously in a hurry, don't do this!)

- Send a follow up email a week after a support session asking how things are going

- Based on your knowledge of how a user works, send an email offering a shortcut or tip chosen especially for that user

- Send a handwritten thank you note to a user for using your support services. Include your business card in the envelope.

Important note: Always be sensitive to your customers or users situation. For example, if they're obviously under a deadline or otherwise in a hurry, just deliver the service, ask if you've solved the problem and if there is anything else they want, thank them, and excuse yourself. You can always go back at a more convenient time to deliver the extra bits of service.

Lagniappe *(pronounced LAN-yap)* is a small gift given to a customer at the time of a purchase. It is a term mainly associated with Louisiana, but it is applicable worldwide. Lagniappe is that little something extra. What are you giving your users (your customers) for lagniappe?

Two Sample
IT Support Calls

Whether you work in IT support or some other form of customer service, review the following two call examples and reflect on what is done poorly and what is done well.

Call Example #1

Read through the transcript of this support call. Analyze the effectiveness of this interaction by answering the questions that follow the transcript. Be prepared to share your insights.

IT Support Staffer: "IT"

User: "Hi, I'm having trouble getting my reports to print out."

IT Support Staffer: "Employee number?"

User: "Sure, it's 123456. I'm wondering; is it me or the computer that is causing the problem?"

IT Support Staffer: [long silence] "What module are you looking at?"

User: "Well, it's the A/R module of the financial package. I'm running the aging report, and I can see it on the screen, but it won't print. I'm really beginning to wonder if my computer is jinxed!"

IT Support Staffer: [long silence] "OK, bud, it's fixed now. Call back if it doesn't work?"

User: "OK, well, I guess that's OK. I'll call back if it isn't working. Bye."

IT Support Staffer: "Later."

Call Example #1 Analysis

- Was the problem fixed to the user's satisfaction?

- Did the IT support staffer's approach show professionalism?

- Did the IT support staffer take advantage of opportunities to connect with the user?

- How do you think the IT support staffer's approach came across to the user? What techniques were used?

- Did the IT support staffer do the best job possible during this interaction?

- If not, what could be done differently?

Call Example #2

Read through the transcript of this new and improved support call. Analyze the effectiveness of this interaction by answering the questions that follow the transcript. Be prepared to share your insights.

IT Support Staffer: "Computer Services. This is Sean. How may I help you?"

User: "Hi, I'm having trouble getting my reports to print out."

IT Support Staffer: "That's strange. I'd be glad to help you with that problem, and I need to start with some basics. Can I have your employee number so I can look up your record?"

User: "Sure, it's 123456. I'm wondering; is it me or the computer that is causing the problem?"

IT Support Staffer: [chuckling] "Well, I sometimes wonder that same thing about my car in the morning. Could you tell me what module you are looking at?"

User: "Well, it's the A/R module of the financial package. I'm running the aging report and I can see it on the screen, but it won't print. I'm really beginning to wonder if my computer is jinxed!"

IT Support Staffer: "I doubt that the computer is jinxed, because I can see that the printer queue is stalled, and it looks like I can start it from here. Give me just a moment, please. I'm not ignoring you. *[Silence for about 20 seconds]* OK, it's fixed now. Why don't you try it while I'm on the phone to make sure it's working?"

User: OK, well, here goes. Oh, great, here comes the report! Wow, that's great. You've been a terrific help. Thanks."

IT Support Staffer: "My pleasure. Is there anything else I can help with today?"

User: "No, I'm all set. And thanks again."

IT Support Staffer: "You're welcome. Call whenever you need us. Goodbye."

Call Example #2 Analysis

- Was the problem fixed to the user's satisfaction?

- Did the IT support staffer's approach show professionalism?

- Did the IT support staffer take advantage of opportunities to connect with the user? What techniques were used?

- How do you think the IT support staffer's approach came across to the user?

- How can you use these techniques in your own IT support work?

Do People Ever Accuse You of Being Rude, Even When You're Not?

I had a conversation with a client who told me he sometimes hears complaints from his end users that he's being rude. He told me that he didn't feel like he was being rude at all.

I doubt he was being rude, but I suspect he maintains a "strictly business" demeanor around the office. I've noticed in our email exchanges and phone calls that his responses to me are terse with no trace of humanness. He's really beyond formal, in that his emails don't even include a greeting ("Hi Don" or "Dear Don"), a complimentary close ("Kind regards" or "Sincerely"), or even an email signature. I noticed in our phone conversations that he didn't initiate any sort of attempt to connect with me as one person to another. Of course, I'm seen as a vendor and sometimes treated differently from, say, co-workers. Still, I wonder if a clue to his problem with end users might be found in the way he interacted with me.

When we're dealing with customers or end users, we've got to remember that we're dealing with another human being. Human beings have feelings. Humans often have a need to feel connected to another human. For many people, it's important to like the people they deal with in the workplace, in stores, healthcare, education, and any other place. Sure, some people don't care about that, but a lot of people do and when we fail to take an extra moment to connect with our fellow humans, we can seem off-putting, uncaring, and even rude, even though our very honorable intention is to simply get the job done. You'd think they'd appreciate our efficiency!

Here are some things you can do:

- **Review Past Emails**. Go back and look at your email exchanges with everyone from customers to co-workers to vendors. If they are "strictly business," consider softening them just a little with things like:

  — A courtesy greeting: "Hi Susan" or "Hello Jim"

  — The more formal greeting: "Dear Robert"

  — A courtesy close: "Sincerely," "Yours truly," or "Kind regards"

  — Even a personal connection comment: "I hope your Monday is going well."

  Please don't misunderstand me on this. I'm suggesting a brief comment to connect on a human-to-human level. I'm certainly not suggesting that we should get deeply personal in business emails!

- **Add a Signature**. Add an email signature with your name, phone number, and email. Consider including your company name and title. It shows you care enough to make yourself easily accessible.

- **Review Your Phone Calls**. Record and review your telephone conversations. (Make sure to let the other parties to the conversations know they're being recorded.) Listening to yourself can be painful sometimes, but it's also a great way to hear yourself the way others hear you.

- **Conduct a Survey**. Consider conducting a survey of your existing end users or customers using a tool such as SurveyMonkey to gather information about how you are perceived. A word of caution on this: You need to be thick-skinned because sometimes the responses you'll receive can be brutal. Only do this if you're really serious about self-improvement and can take criticism without becoming defensive.

- **Smile!** A smile comes through even in telephone conversations. It adds warmth to your voice and makes you seem friendlier and more approachable. Consider putting a small mirror on your desk to remind you to smile when you're on the phone.

Always remember that we're dealing with people and must find ways to make our communications human with a touch of warmth and our own humanness.

SOUNDTHINKING POINT:
Too Formal or Too Casual?

There is a shifting line that exists between being too formal and too casual in dealing with other people. It shifts based on the people with whom we're dealing. It's important for us to measure how our customer or user prefers to be treated and respect that. Some people prefer interactions with us to be strictly business, while others may prefer a more casual interaction. A good guideline is to mirror the actions of the person you're dealing with while always maintaining an attitude of friendly professionalism.

FOR REFLECTION AND DISCUSSION

Have you ever dealt with someone who was "strictly business" in their demeanor? Did you feel a connection with that person? If not, what could he or she have done to create a human connection with you?

Do you ever find yourself thinking negative thoughts or dwelling on the negative things in your life? How does that affect the things you say to those around you? What about your actions? Are they affected by your negative thoughts?

Has anyone ever tried to be funny with you, but ended up saying something unintentionally hurtful? How did that make you feel?

To-Dos

Create an email signature including your name, title, and contact information.

Review your email exchanges to see if you might be coming across as unnecessarily cold, brusque, or even rude.

Try to be more aware during your next support session of how the other person is reacting to you. See if there are some things you can do to be more understanding and reassuring.

Think about what you can do to give your customer or user a "baker's dozen." Maybe it's printing out a tip sheet for the software or product you support. Some people keep small chocolates to share with co-workers or customers.

Consider setting up a wiki to consolidate and share information.

CHAPTER SIX:

THE CHALLENGE OF DIFFERENT GENERATIONS

*"Blessed is the generation in which the old listen to the young; and doubly blessed
is the generation in which the young listen to the old"*

—Talmud

In their landmark book *Generations at Work*, authors Ron Zemke, Claire
Raines, and Bob Filipczak make the case that our year of birth is a
powerfully influential factor in how each of us views our world. (Zemke,
Raines and Filipczak 1999) As people who serve other people, we can use
that knowledge to craft our interactions based on the approximate age of the
person with whom we're dealing.

As you read through this chapter, think about the people in your workplace.
Think about how you might treat them differently if you have a better
understanding of how each of them views their world.

Today's workplace has greater diversity among its employees than at any other
time in our history. Until recently, it seemed as though we managed a fairly
homogeneous group of people, meaning they were all about the same age and
sex with similar racial/ethnic backgrounds and equally similar socio/cultural

environments. It required only a few tools and just a moderate understanding of these issues to function well in a workplace team. But today the situation is radically changed: Your team is very likely composed of men and women of all age groups with differing racial/ethnic/cultural backgrounds as well as widely ranging socio/economic backgrounds. In this chapter, you will examine the way people of different age groups look at the world, the workplace, and technology.

- What are the four generational groups at work?

- How have world and national events shaped their view of the workplace?

- Where do the loyalties of each group lie?

- To which group do the IT managers belong?

- Who are the IT support professionals?

- What are the potential pitfalls dealing with each group?

GENERATIONS IN THE WORKPLACE

Researchers say that today there are four distinct generations in the U.S. workplace, based on year of birth. Although there have always been different age groups working throughout our history, world events of the twentieth century and the change from a largely agrarian and industrial society to one of technology has impacted the U.S. work environment like no other in the world. As a result, four "work generations" have emerged, each with their own view towards the world, and especially the workplace. Understanding these differences can help support managers and front-line support staff recognize potential areas of conflict and be better prepared to deal with them. Such an understanding can help both in creating workplace harmony as well as in dealing with customers and end users.

HISTORICAL EVENTS
AND THE GENERATIONS

To start our understating of the generations, it is worth looking at historical events in a timeline. Our individual worldview is largely shaped by the environment in which we grew up and the lessons we learned from our parents, relatives, teachers, neighbors, and friends.

A successful radio station programming consultant observed that the popular music of your teenage and early post-teen years becomes "the music of your life." Similarly, the events taking place during our formative years can shape our view of our world, from our families to our communities to our nation and world. (That same consultant also observed that each generation needs a music form that their parents can't stand. Think of Sinatra, Elvis, the Beatles, and Snoop Dog as examples. When an older person describes a younger person's music by saying things like, "That's not music!" or "That stuff hurts my ears!" it's a good indication of generationally specific music.)

Human Beings Are Unique

Like much research into human behavior, the descriptions of generational differences are stereotypes and cannot, and should not, be applied with absolute certainty—but they are a good place to begin.

The bullet list on the next page shows some of the major influencers by decade. What are some of the things you recall from your adolescent and teenage years? For example, members of the Veterans generation can tell you exactly where they were and what they were doing when the Japanese attacked Pearl Harbor. Baby Boomers can tell you exactly where they were and what they were doing when President Kennedy was shot. Certainly, members of all generations recall where they were and what they were doing when the World Trade Center was attacked. The attack is a defining moment, however, for the Millennial generation. Identifying a defining moment for Gen Xers has been difficult for generational researchers. In a non-scientific study of several Gen Xers, individuals mentioned things, such as the death of Lady Di or Kurt Cobain's suicide, but there was not general agreement on a single defining moment.

The following list shows some of the significant events that occurred during the past eight decades:

- **1930s:** Stock Market Crash, Great Depression, Election of FDR

- **1940s:** Pearl Harbor, D-Day, Death of FDR, First use of atomic weapons, end of World War II, start of the Cold War

- **1950s:** McCarthy hearings, Korean War, television, Elvis Presley and the start of Rock 'n Roll, polio vaccine introduced, Brown vs. Board of Education

- **1960s:** Vietnam, Kennedy elected, civil rights movement, Kennedy/King assassinations, space race and moon landing, Cold War intensification, Cuban missile crisis, Woodstock, the Beatles, birth control pill

- **1970s:** Oil embargo, Watergate, Nixon resignation, appearance of PCs, Roe vs. Wade, women's rights, Iran hostage situation, rap/hip-hop music

- **1980s:** Fall of Berlin Wall, Challenger disaster, John Lennon killed, Reagan elected, Iran contra scandal

- **1990s:** Desert Storm, Oklahoma City bombing, Clinton scandals, death of Princess Diana

- **2000s:** Election of President George W. Bush, World Trade Center attack, Iraq war, Election of President Barack Obama, Pope John Paul II dies

- **2010s:** Global economic collapse, Arab Spring, reelection of Barack Obama, Resignation of Pope Benedict, Election of Pope Francis, U.S. Supreme Court rulings on major social issues including marriage equality

By reviewing the preceding list as we consider the generations in today's workforce, it is possible to identify some clues as to why they are the way they are. Different authors use slightly different years as divisional points. They are, for the most part, a matter of convenience for discussion, and in no case did the characteristics of the individual generations change overnight.

1922 – 1943: The Veterans

Most, but certainly not all, of the workers in this generation have left the workplace at the time of this writing (summer 2013), but for a variety of reasons, many older workers are choosing to remain in the workforce long past traditional retirement ages.

This group of workers has been referred to as the Veterans, GI Generation, Radio Generation, and the Silent Generation. The older members of this generation grew up coming out of the American economic depression. Younger members grew up during the recovery from World War II. Because they and their parents endured the hardships of much higher unemployment, they learned that getting and keeping a job required obeying bosses and other people in positions of power. Because the available labor pool was fairly large, a management technique that worked with this generation was "my way or the highway," which contributed to them being known as the "silent generation." As a group they are very steady and reliable workers. They show up for work early and go home late. Their loyalty is to the company, and it was not uncommon for them to be with the same firm their entire career.

The Veterans generation has observed the pace of technology increase throughout their lives. When they were children, America was a strong mix of agrarian and industrial work environments. The type of labor required was primarily manual. As they progressed through their careers, they saw technology change from requiring a few basic hand tools and a modicum of common sense to fix almost anything, to an era of specialized equipment and knowledge for almost every task. (Think about the changes in automobile maintenance during their lives!) They are not change-phobic, but they can be intimidated and confused by rapid change. They can and do want to use computers as a work tool, but require more time to learn programs. Because they are focused on getting things done they tend to be less interested in knowing multiple ways of accomplishing the same task. They tend to prefer a consistent environment.

1943 – 1960: Baby Boomers

Baby Boomers grew up in the relative prosperity of an America transformed by the Veterans. They too learned from their parents what would be considered a strong work ethic, but also believed there was more to life than just work. They came of age in a world of improving communications and technology with the advent of television and electric everything. The early boomers were on the leading edge of the civil rights movement, and were significantly impacted by the Kennedy/King assassinations, Vietnam War, and Watergate/Nixon scandals. One result was that they coined the phrase "trust no one over thirty." In various degrees they became anti-establishment. One of the results of this is that their loyalty moved from the company to themselves. They are good team players, but in the end they tend to be more interested in "what's in it for me."

Boomers tend to be work-aholics and play-aholics. They work hard, play hard, and have lots of toys. They are always on the move with lives full of activity. They can easily burn themselves out. They can be motivated by power, position, and prestige. They saw the beginnings of and endured the downsizing of corporate America, losing their jobs for no other reason than being in the wrong place at the wrong time.

1960 – 1980: Generation X

As children of the late Veterans and the Boomers, Generation X members mark a significant change in attitude towards the workplace. They grew up in an era of increasing technology and became very adept with it. In fact, this is the generation in which we see a role reversal regarding technology. They understand and know more about its use than their parents.

As a group they tend to be independent, cynical, and highly mobile. For the most part, they raised themselves as "latchkey kids" since their parents both worked. They saw their parents lose their jobs for what seemed no logical reason and learned to not trust the company. Who they do trust are their friends and siblings, and that is where their loyalties lie—to those relationships. They have little interest in spending the bulk of their time in the workplace. In fact, they work to live and will job hop in order to achieve that end. They are quite resistant to "my way or the highway" or "doing things by the book." They want to understand the reasons why things are done the way they are.

They may build very close relationships with their co-workers and work place behaviors can include taking breaks together, "doing lunch" together, and socializing with each other in the evenings and on weekends. This tight bonding can and has led to the entire team quitting when only one of them is upset or perceives mistreatment by the organization. The lower unemployment is in a sector, or the higher the demand for a scarce technical skill-set, the higher the probability there is of this occurring.

1980 – Present: The Millennials

The final generation currently identified in the workplace is the Millennials, sometimes referred to as Generation Y or the Nexters. At the time of this writing (2013), the older Millennials have started moving into middle management positions. The Millennials are quite familiar with collaboration tools and often have little or no patience for workplaces that don't support or encourage the use of such tools.

It is very important to remember that these descriptions are stereotypes. In fact, your birth year may qualify you as, say, a Baby Boomer, yet you may exhibit characteristics of a Millennial. The Pew Research Center even has a 14 question quiz available online titled How Millennial Are You? (*http://www. pewresearch.org/quiz/how-millennial-are-you/*). (I'm a Baby Boomer by birth year, but my score on the quiz put me at the older end of Gen X.)

Although the groups' characteristics trend into these categories, there are many individual exceptions. For example, employees who grew up in rural areas, and in particular on a farm or ranch, will have what many consider a strong work ethic regardless of year of birth. Those who grew up in major metropolitan areas seem to fall more strongly into the described categories, but here again, there are exceptions. And finally, there is evidence that some people shift their workplace attitude as they age. As an example, some of the boomers are adopting attitudes more like those of Gen X.

COMMUNICATING WITH THE GENERATIONS

Regardless of the generation with whom you are communicating, here are some universal communication guidelines:

- Be respectful, never condescending.

- Keep it professional, avoid pet phrases and slang (even when you know someone well, it is best to keep such language out of the workplace). Although this suggestion may seem stilted, there is no harm in maintaining a friendly but professional demeanor in the workplace. There is, however, great potential for career harm in being perceived as too casual and unprofessional in the workplace.

- Individualize your approach based on the person you're communicating with. Notice how he or she communicates with you and mirror that style. If you're unsure, ask what this individual's preference is. (This doesn't mean, however, that a 50-something should attempt to use the same language as a 20-something. That can be perceived as phony, silly, and even condescending.)

- Respect the other person's time.

- Realize that different people have different values. Make an effort to understand and respect those values, even if you don't agree with them.

- Don't make assumptions about other people. If you're uncertain how another person views a particular issue, ask!

- Be patient with each other.

- Don't take yourself too seriously.

Again, Human Beings Are Unique

As mentioned earlier, these are guidelines and certainly not hard-and-fast rules. First and foremost, remember that you are dealing with human beings, each of whom brings a unique set of experiences and expectations to his interaction with you. The following guidelines provide a starting point for choosing a communication style, based on generational memberships. You can also ask the individual how he or she would prefer you communicate with him or her.

Also, remember that understanding is a two-way street.

Regardless, you'll rarely go wrong by maintaining an air of friendly, kind, and respectful professionalism.

Communicating with Veterans (Traditionalists)

- Use face-to-face or written communication.

- Members of this generation tend to be more private, so don't expect them to immediately share their thoughts or feelings.

- Older generations communicated more formally during the first years of their career. They may be uncomfortable with a Gen X or Gen Y casual communication style.

- They will tend to pay more attention to the words you say than to your gestures and other forms of body language. Choose your words wisely!

- Veterans tend to prefer face-to-face communication or talking on the phone instead of texting, instant messaging, or email.

Communicating with Baby Boomers

- Show flexibility by presenting options.

- Be open and direct, but not controlling or manipulating.

- Give complete, thorough answers to questions and expect follow up questions.

- Like Veterans, Boomers tend to prefer face-to-face communication or talking on the phone instead of texting, instant messaging, or email.

Communicating with Generation Xers

- Use an informal communication style (while maintaining professionalism).

- Email should be your first choice for communication.

- Use short sound bites to communicate and keep their attention.

- Be inclusive; share information frequently.

- Be prepared to give and receive feedback.

- Gen Xers tend to prefer text-based communication forms, such as texting, instant messaging, and email. Do NOT leave lengthy voice mail messages for Gen Xers.

- Veterans and Baby Boomers may want to consider making their communication style slightly more casual with Gen Xers.

Communicating with Millennials

- Consider using texting, IMing, Facebook, or even Twitter for communication.

- As with Gen Xers, be prepared to give and receive feedback regularly, and with Millennials provide instant feedback.

- As with Gen Xers, veterans and Baby Boomers may want to consider making their communication style slightly more casual with Millennials.

- Millennials tend to prefer text-based communication forms, such as texting, instant messaging, and, to a lesser extent, email. As with Gen Xers, do NOT leave lengthy voice mail messages for Gen Xers. In fact, Millennials may not even listen to voice mail messages. They may simply notice that you called and return your call without listening to your message.

- Encourage them to try new things and find new ways of learning.

FOR REFLECTION AND DISCUSSION

Think about your recent interactions with people from different generations. How do they see the world differently from you? Is there something to learn from their view of the world compared to yours?

Reflect on your view of the world compared to your parents? What do or did your parents think of your music? What do you think of a different generation's choice of music? Have you ever said the words, "That stuff's not music"?

What were the landmark events that occurred during your formative years? How might those events have affected your view of the world?

Have you ever noticed that particular communication methods don't work with a different generation from yours?

To-Dos

Ask a member of a different generation for a musical suggestion that he or she thinks you might like.

Spend time with a really old person. Spend time with kids.

Spend time socially with someone of a different generation. Go out for a cup of coffee.

Refer to the list of significant events found earlier in this chapter and research events with which you are unfamiliar.

Interview someone from a different generation about their views on work, politics, social issues, morality, and society.

Take the Pew Research Center's quiz to determine *How Millennial Are You?* and, in the process, learn a lot about some of the criteria used to describe the Millennial generation.

118

CHAPTER SEVEN

COMMUNICATING THROUGH EMAIL, TEXTING, AND INSTANT MESSAGING

"Diamonds are forever. E-mail comes close."

—June Kronholz

More and more communication today takes place through some form of a written medium, whether it's via email, texting, or chat. Done correctly, it can be very effective and efficient. Done incorrectly, it can be maddening for your customer or end user. In this chapter, I'll give you some ideas on how to handle written communication correctly and also provide some examples of how not to do it.

COMMUNICATING THROUGH EMAIL

Email is often the most commonly used form of communication for support professionals. Email is a one-dimensional form of communication, which, although efficient, fails to account for human emotions as a vital component of communication. (Other forms of written communication, including texting, instant messaging, and even old-fashioned letter writing suffer from the same limitation.)

In order for your customer or user to know you care, there are several important rules to follow when communicating via email (many of these tips also apply to live chat or texting sessions):

1. Use a descriptive and specific subject line that will help you and the user identify this particular email conversation in the future. Many support ticketing systems automatically add a ticket number. If yours doesn't, consider adding a ticket number manually.

2. Personalize your response by including the user's name.

3. Reread the sender's original email to ensure that you're answering all of his questions and haven't inadvertently overlooked any of the issues in the email. (Have you ever experienced the frustration of receiving only a partial response to an inquiry and having to send another email requesting answers to questions that were ignored from your first email?)

4. Never assume that the customer or user has a particular level of knowledge. It is much better to be too thorough than to omit necessary steps because you assume the person receiving your email already knows something.

5. Anticipate related issues that the user or customer might have and include links to support pages or, if necessary, steps for the recipient to follow if she encounters any related issues.

6. Bullet-point your response to make it easier to read. Long paragraphs are difficult to digest, and it's easy to miss interior points buried in lengthy blocks of text.

7. If your response includes step-by-step instructions, be sure to number them. If you're creating such instructions from scratch, be sure to test them to ensure you haven't omitted any steps or made false assumptions about how the steps should work. (As a person who has written a ton of technical documentation, I'm speaking from personal experience on this!)

8. Show professionalism by using proper grammar and avoiding the use of texting shortcuts (they're fine for personal use but have no place in business)

9. Additionally, show professionalism by proofreading for meaning, spelling, grammar, and mechanical errors, such as repeated keystrokes or incorrect spelling (just get in the habit of rereading every email completely before hitting the send button).

10. Use emoticons to express or to clarify emotions (but be careful about their overuse). Also be sensitive as to who will be reading your email. You probably wouldn't, for example, put a smiley face in an email to the CEO or other C-level executives of your company!

11. Ensure your contact information is included in every email. Automated signature features in most email programs make this very easy. Include your name, phone number, email address, office hours, and appropriate links, such as your company or department website, support pages, and any work-related social networking sites, such as LinkedIn.

EMAIL SUPPORT EXAMPLES

The following are some examples showing screen captures of email correspondence to either avoid or emulate.

Take 1: A Rotten Response

In the first screen capture below, notice how the support person, Bill, seems to take a cavalier attitude toward the user and her problem. He displays unprofessionalism by using texting abbreviations and poor grammar and spelling (spelling "your" when he means "you're"), assuming she knows how to make the change to IMAP, and not providing contact information.

Figure 0.1:
A really bad email response
to a support ticket

Take 2: A Right-On Response

Now, let's switch to the other end of the spectrum. In the following example this time, our support staffer Bill follows the above rules by:

- Providing a descriptive subject line

- Calling the user by name

- Repeating back his understanding of the problem

- Anticipating other problems the user might not have seen (such as the program not being installed)

- Using headers to segment the problem resolution sections

- Numbering the steps

- Using an emoticon to relieve any possible anxiety over the word "advanced"

- Providing contact information including office hours

- Providing a website with additional information.

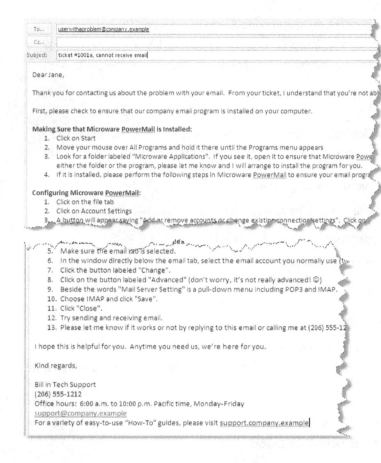

Figure 0.2:
The top
half of a
good email
response

Figure 0.3:
The bottom
half of a
good email
response

COMMONLY MISUSED AND ABUSED WORDS

Is grammar important? To some people, it doesn't matter at all. For others, however, it's very important. Below are some common grammar, usage, and spelling errors that can make you look unprofessional and incompetent.

Is this being nit-picky? Maybe, but if you're applying for a job with an HR manager or working with a customer for whom grammar and spelling matter, you can sink your chances by making one of these mistakes. Proper grammar, spelling, and usage is really important for some people. It's not worth taking a chance when the following rules are fairly easy to learn and remember.

Your vs. You're

You're is a contraction (or combination) of the words *you* and *are*. *Your* is the possessive form of *you*. (Hint: *Your* is interchangeable with *my*.)

> Correct: You're very good at grammar.
>
> *Incorrect*: Your expected to be at work on time.
>
> Correct: Your parents are coming for a visit.
>
> *Incorrect*: You're car ran out of gas.

There, Their, and They're

Use *there* when referring to a place or with verbs such as *is, are, was,* and *were.* Use *their* to indicate plural possession. *They're* is a contraction of the words *they* and *are*.

> Correct: I'm excited to go there.
>
> *Incorrect*: I've never been their before.
>
> Correct: Did you see their beautiful gardens?
>
> *Incorrect*: They're house has a stone entryway.
>
> Correct: They're going to the opera tonight.
>
> Incorrect: There two of my favorite people

Accept vs. Except

Accept is to agree or to receive. *Except* is a synonym for *but*, an exception.

Correct: I'm delighted to accept your invitation.

Incorrect: I can't except your money.

Correct: I like all animals except snakes.

Incorrect: My favorite dessert is ice cream, accept vanilla.

Affect vs. Effect

Use *effect* when you're talking about a result. It's also used when you're talking about causing something to happen. Use *affect* when you're talking about influencing rather than causing.

Correct: I wonder how the rain will affect the water level in the lake.

Incorrect: Will his mistake effect his career?

Correct: The special lighting produced a nice effect.

Incorrect: The chiles added a spicy affect.

All right vs. Alright

Strunk and White say, *all right* is "properly written as two words." *Alright* is commonly used though and will probably become accepted usage in the near future. For now, however, the recommended usage is *all right*.

Correct: It's all right. Don't worry about it.

Incorrect: Alright, I'll take care of it.

Assure, Ensure, or Insure

To *assure* is to say or promise something with confidence. To *ensure* is to make certain that something will or won't happen. To *insure* is to issue an insurance policy.

> Correct: I can assure you of his integrity.

> *Incorrect*: We want to insure your safety. (Unless you have a financial interest in their safety, you probably don't want to insure it!)

> Correct: It's important to ensure your children are given proper guidance.

> Correct: It's important to insure your home against loss.

I vs. Me

Use *I* when it is the subject of a verb. For example, "Jen and I scheduled the training." In this sentence, *Jen* and *I* are the subjects of the verb *scheduled*, so the correct usage is *I*. Saying "Jen and me" is incorrect. Use *me* when it is the object of a verb. The object of a verb typically follows the verb and is affected by or receives some action. Take the example, "Tom sent a gift certificate to Janet and me." In this example, *Janet* and *me* are the objects of the verb *sent*, so *me* is the correct usage. An easy way to check yourself is to remove the proper nouns from the sentence. In the first example, you would say "I scheduled the training," not "Me scheduled the training." In the second example, you would say "Tom sent a gift certificate to me," not "Tom sent a gift certificate to I." Also, remember that *I* and *me* go after other nouns and pronouns.

> Correct: Janet and I are excited to see you.

> *Incorrect*: We're excited for you to join Janet and I for the holidays.

> Correct: Jared and I are getting together tonight after work.

> *Incorrect*: Me and Jared are getting together tonight after work.

Its vs. It's

The thing to remember is that *it's* is always a contraction of the words *it is* or *it has*. It's never used to indicate possession. It's frequently misused. When misused, its meaning changes.

Correct: It's time to go home.

Incorrect: The cat lost it's hat.

Correct: The statue fell off its pedestal.

Incorrect: Seattle is known for it's rain.

Loose vs. Lose

Loose means not tight. To *lose* something means it is *lost*.

Irregardless

Irregardless is not a word. Just say *regardless*.

SOUNDTHINKING POINT:
What's the Point of Using Proper Grammar and Spelling?

I read an article in which the writer suggested that we, as a society, need to lighten up on the rules for grammar and spelling. While he makes an excellent case for worrying less about such things, he also misses an important point. When you're trying to build a career or please a customer, perceptions can make the difference between getting a promotion or having a satisfied customer. As mentioned above, for some people proper spelling and grammar is very important. It's so easy to avoid common grammar and usage errors that it's simply not worth taking a chance.

REFERENCES

- *The Elements of Style* by William Strunk, Jr. and E.B. White
- *The Chicago Manual of Style, 16th Edition*, University of Chicago Press Staff (Editor)
- *www.grammarbook.com*

COMMUNICATING VIA TEXTING

(txtng: a gr8 way 2 communic8 … maybe)

Know Who Is on the Other End

For some people who are good at texting, it is a very natural and comfortable way to communicate, while for others, texting is one of the most unnatural and uncomfortable acts of modern times. Texting can be a very efficient method of communication when done between two people who are both proficient. When one person is uncomfortable with it, however, it can hinder communication or, worse, prevent any communication from happening.

Text Transmissions Are Not 100 Percent Reliable

Another consideration in texting is the technical reliability of the process. Because the successful transmission of text messages is dependent upon cellular carriers' networks, the sending and receiving of text message transmissions is not 100 percent reliable. Most of us have, at some point, sent text messages that weren't received until hours or even days later. In fact, I just checked my phone and noticed a text message I tried to send to a relative two weeks ago still hasn't been sent.

Texting Can Be Expensive

Some people don't include text messaging in their cell phone plans. For them, texting can get very expensive very quickly. Obviously, you should avoid sending them text messages and use email, phone calls, or voice messaging instead. This really goes back to what I mentioned in the section about communicating with different generations: Individualize your communication to match the preference of the recipient.

Texting Is Great for Short Messages

The technical term for texting is SMS or Short Message Service. It's great for quick messages, but not for involved conversations.

Good Uses of Texting

- To let someone know you're on your way

- To let someone know you're delayed and your approximate time of arrival

- To set up a meeting time

- To check on availability for a phone call

- To set a meeting place

- To ask quick questions requiring only a short answer

- To send a quick update (for example, "The server is going down for maintenance at midnight.")

Bad Uses of Texting

- When driving or doing other things that require your attention

- When in a meeting or social gathering with other people (it's just rude)

- When the other person is uncomfortable with it or doesn't include it in his/her cell plan

- Lengthy conversations

- Anything requiring a lot of typing

Be careful about the use of abbreviations, especially those for which the definition is inappropriate for the workplace. If the abbreviations stand for words that are usually considered profane, don't use them in work-related text messages. Even innocuous abbreviations like LOL, BRB, or JK are not as widely known as we may think. (If you're not someone who uses texting or instant messaging, LOL means "laughing out loud," BRB means "be right back," and JK means "just kidding.")

COMMUNICATING VIA INSTANT MESSAGING (IMING)

Instant messaging (or chat) is frequently used for customer support. It offers many benefits, including the ability to transfer files and send the end user a transcript of the support session.

The rules for polite conversation also apply to IM conversations:

- Introduce yourself and include your contact information at the beginning of the session

- As with texting, think short. Although IM is more conducive to long conversations than texting, briefer is still better. If what you need to say won't fit in the chat window without scrolling, consider using email instead.

- Be careful what you write. As with email, anything you say in a chat session can be saved and circulated.

- Give the other person time to respond. Some people type more slowly than others. Sometimes, distractions prevent an immediate response. Remember that conversations are a give-and-take process. Let the other person respond before you send additional messages.

- Keep it light and professional. Chat sessions are not the place to criticize a user (or anyone else, for that matter). They are great for walking users and customers step-by-step through a procedure, for sending out quick informational updates, and for answering user questions.

- Be careful about using common chat and texting abbreviations. As mentioned above, while you might think BRB or LOL are universally known, they are not. In the same way that you would avoid slang and jargon during in-person encounters, the same idea applies in chat sessions.

- Since chat sessions are emotionless, it can be desirable to use emoticons (such as an occasional smiley face) during sessions. Do so sparingly and with an awareness of who the person is on the other end of the chat session. For example, you probably don't want to use emoticons with an upper-level executive.

- Write your chat messages in a professional manner. It is easy to get in a hurry and rush through sessions, especially during a hectic workday. Be careful, however, about spelling and grammar in chat. Poor spelling and grammar can actually change the meaning of what is being said, sometimes with unintended consequences.

- If you often receive support requests via chat, be sure to use an away message when you have stepped away from your desk. Consider including in the message your anticipated time of return.

 SOUNDTHINKING POINT:
Exclamation Marks and Upper-Case

Exclamation points are used to indicate a high-level of excitement. (The Chicago Manual of Style says they mark outcries or emphatic or ironic comments.) Avoid the use of exclamation points except to show that you're really excited. Never use more than one exclamation mark! (Yes, I'm excited about this.)

TYPING IN ALL UPPER-CASE IS CONSIDERED SHOUTING. DON'T DO IT. Besides, it's just really hard to read.

FOR REFLECTION AND DISCUSSION

Consider your text exchanges. Are you trying to text with people who might prefer another means of communication?

Think about the last time you tried to find contact information for a business contact, but there was nothing in any of your communications to help.

Have you ever dealt with a support rep who assumed you had a particular level of knowledge, but you didn't?

Have you ever dealt with a support rep who used very casual language and shortcuts in a business setting? Did that feel right to you?

Think about any pet peeves you have that may not bother other people. Might those pet peeves influence your decision if you were in a position to hire someone?

To-Dos

Create a customized email signature for the bottom of all your emails. Include your basic contact information, office hours, and other information that your end users or customers can use to simplify the process of contacting you or otherwise obtaining support.

Review past emails and written communication for grammar and spelling errors. Looking at past mistakes can help prevent new ones.

Ask a colleague to review some of your past emails for grammar and spelling errors.

Review the above section on commonly misused and abused words to ensure you don't make those common errors.

CHAPTER EIGHT

HOW TO SAY "NO" WITHOUT ALIENATING YOUR END USER

"Good judgment comes from experience, and experience—
well that comes from poor judgment."

—Aesop

I have a friend who works in a law firm as a legal assistant. When she first started there, the office manager came up to her and said, "We try to never say 'no' to our clients." My friend thought, "But, what if the answer is 'no'?" I think we often get carried away with good ideas that become workplace clichés. This is a great example. Of course we want to find ways to accommodate our customers, but that doesn't mean we never say "no." In my friend's case, what if someone asked if she were an attorney? The only legal and ethical answer is "no." I hope that what her office manager really meant was something like this: "We try to never say "no" without offering an alternative." That makes sense, and that's what this chapter is all about.

Sometimes, what the customer or end user wants simply can't be done. When that happens, the skillful support staffer delivers the news in a way that is clear, yet non-offensive. Offer alternatives, if available, but the key lies in finding a way to say "no" without leaving the end user feeling neglected or ignored.

- The art of no

- Dealing with the unsolvable problem

- Getting end-user buy-in

- What to do when you don't know or can't find the answer

THE CUSTOMER SERVICE CHALLENGE

When your job is to support end users and customers, it is hard to say "no" to some end user or customer requests that come your way. Customer service is all about helping people and solving problems, and, from the user's or customer's perspective, that implies that you will go out of your way to accept any and all requests. A primary role of support centers is to serve and support end users and customers, and that involves solving problems and filling needs as requested. But you have to serve more than just individual customer or end-user needs—you also have to serve company interests, professional ethics, and technology best practices. For example, end users may believe they would have an easier time of it if they could ignore security measures and do away with user IDs and passwords, but doing so would certainly not be in the best interest of the organization. (Frankly, it's not in the users' or customers' best interests either when you consider the embarrassment of hacked email accounts.) Sometimes, workplace interests or policies must take priority over end-user interests, and you may need to say "no," even if you are technically capable of fulfilling the request.

WHEN TO SAY "NO" TO AN END USER OR CUSTOMER?

Not all issues that require a "no" answer are security-related. There are other things to consider and questions you should ask yourself before you agree to help someone when the request is not common and ordinary. For example:

- Do you have the time to complete the request? You may have a genuine desire and willingness to help fulfill a special request, but not enough time.

- Does your schedule allow you to spend time on a custom solution for one user?

- Do you have the resources to complete the request? You may be inundated with requests that have a higher priority and cannot ask for help to fulfill the request. In this case, you may have to say "no," at least temporarily.

- Are you qualified to complete the request? You may have a genuine desire to help and would like to learn more about a certain tool or technique, but you may not presently have the skills to complete the request.

- Do you have the authority to fulfill this request? You may have been given instructions not to take on certain types of requests. Sometimes end users and customers can ask you to go above and beyond what your policies and procedures recommend.

- Are you really authorized to abandon the policies that are in place? What might the consequences be if you do?

- Is the request within the scope of your responsibilities?

Giving yourself an honest answer to these questions sometimes leads you to the conclusion that you must say "no" in some circumstances, regardless of how much you want to help someone or how skilled you are.

When you must refuse an end user or customer request, you want to do so without an outright "no" response. If you are abrupt or alienate your end users and customers, they may bypass you in the future, complain about you, or just go over your head. So the art here is to say "no" in a way that is neither brusque, nor off-putting and which leaves your customer or user feeling that their needs have been heard and met to the best of your ability. This can be accomplished carefully, but not unless you have thoroughly examined all of the factors that may affect your decision to reject the request.

SOUNDTHINKING POINT:
Speak Like a Normal Human

There's a seafood store near my home in Seattle where I frequently shop. I recently stopped there looking for large clams to barbeque. When I asked the clerk about Cherrystone clams, he loudly and brusquely replied, "That's a negative!" So, I asked if he had Horse clams. Again, the same terse response, "That's a negative!" He didn't ask if there was anything else I wanted or if there was any other way he could help. He basically shut me down with his rude response and missed an opportunity to perhaps sell me a different kind of seafood. It was odd that he chose to use a two-way radio form of communication with a customer, but it was just bad business for him not to engage with me to find out if there was some other product that might have worked for me or if there was anything else I needed.

CONSIDERATIONS BEFORE SAYING "NO"

Consider Who Is Making the Service Request

Before you turn down a service request, you need to consider "who is asking?" Because of someone's rank or political status in the organization, you may not be able to say "no," even if "no" is the right answer. Think twice before saying "yes" in these circumstances, though, because you should not promise to handle an issue that you can't follow through on. Sometimes, you need to get more information or talk to your manager or get advice before providing an answer to someone. You only have so many hours in the day, and saying "yes" without thinking it over carefully or consulting with your coworkers or management team may stop you from fulfilling other tasks that are required to do your job adequately.

Listen and Make Sure You Fully Understand the Request

In order to respond to a request properly, you need to make sure you understand the nature and scope of the request, and how it relates to projects already underway, new projects, or workplace initiatives. Let your end users and customers talk, and show them that you are listening by making the appropriate responses, such as suggesting how to solve the problem. If you turn down the request without fully understanding it, you may regret it later and cause your end user to be frustrated.

Evaluate the Request

Evaluate the request in order to determine whether you can and should, or are required to, say "yes," or decide to turn down the request. In your deliberations, you need to consider company policies, priorities you have been given, your schedule, resources, skills, and other related issues.

Craft Your Answer

Considering the type of request information you discovered during your evaluation, you will develop a response that fits into one of the following categories:

- "Yes," you agree to fulfill the request

- "No," with an explanation of reasons you can't complete the request

- An alternative or compromise

- A referral to the name of someone else that is authorized or has the skills and time to fulfill the request.

In cases where you must refuse the request, you need to explain your decision. By taking the time to offer an explanation, the reasons for turning down the request take priority over the rejection itself. This gives you a chance to explain your decision. Giving an explanation could help you later if someone complains about your response. If you just say "no" without an explanation, it would be harder to justify and defend your decision. Your role as a support person is to serve the organization and your end users and customers. If others perceive that you are not serving your users and customers and are refusing requests without just reasons, you may not be in your position for very long.

Offer Your Explanation

How you choose to communicate your response will depend on several factors: The nature of the request (formal or informal), the person making the request, your relationship with that person, the sensitivity of your response, and the culture of your workplace. You may choose to make your response in person, on the phone, through email, or a combination of methods. No matter which method you choose, you should always follow a few basic techniques:

- **Don't be defensive or apologetic**. Simply state that you regret that you cannot complete the request at this time and offer your explanation (time conflicts, conflicts with internal policies, conflicts with other plans or projects, security reasons). Emphasize the reason, not the fact that you are turning down the request. Using the word "because" gives a logical framework to what you are saying, and helps the person receiving the message receive and accept your logic. "I can't help you to create a new login for a temporary worker because it is against security policies." (If the user pushes you on issues such as this, you can always offer to escalate the issue to your supervisor.)

- **Be as positive as possible**. Focus on any compromises or alternatives that you can offer. Always leave yourself an opening for a graceful exit. Your end user may offer an alternative of their own, tell you what they think is wrong with your logic, or react negatively to your response. If necessary, leave yourself a way to "rethink" the matter so that you can seek assistance from your own management. Try a simple statement, such as "If you have any questions, or feel that I have misunderstood your request in any way, please let me know." Let the end user know that you are still open to seeking a workable solution.

Be Proactive

Having to turn down an end user's request can be difficult and stressful. You need the right combination of communication and interpersonal skills to carry it off. The following are some proactive steps to make the process easier:

- Seek advice and guidance from your manager when necessary. At the very least, it is wise to notify your manager if a problem is likely to occur with an unhappy user, or if the user will be contacting the manager. (You never want your manager to be blindsided by an upset end user. If you know a user is going to contact your manager, it is always best that the manager get a "heads up" from you.) Also, when you have to make a difficult decision, you should be able to ask for advice or help as needed.

- Set structured procedures and formats to use when you submit responses to end-user requests. If you establish and enforce a structured process, which may include filling out a form or issuing a ticket number for end-user requests, you will minimize the familiarity associated by being able to ask for special favors or informal demands that you may forget or be unable to follow through on. Using a structured request process will improve your IT support services

- Organize yourself, your schedule, and prioritize your workload for efficiency.

Find Another Way to Say "No"

You are required to serve your users and customers, and it is never easy to say "no." Your challenge is to balance the need to serve multiple end users and customers, with the need to meet overall priorities and serve workplace interests. Sometimes, a "no" is necessary to meet that goal, but it is often not necessary to use that word.

For example, rather than saying "no," you can say that you will have to research and work on their problem further to find a suitable solution. You can also say something like, "We are unable to provide that service," but don't say "no." The word "no" gives rise to too many emotional issues and can put people off.

Some people will ask too much, and at some point, you have to cut them off, but do it without saying "no." In addition, point out all that you have given and all that you have attempted to do to right their problem. Help them accept that they have been taken care of and that you have exhausted all options to solve their problem. Think about how you like to be treated when you call in for support and then deliver that same consideration to your end user. It's how you say "no" that matters.

You can't accommodate everyone, so find or create alternatives. Brainstorm difficult customer service problems with your team. Share each new alternative solution that you come up with that can be used over and over again. Document these solutions and alternatives. A co-worker may have a smooth way of handling something that puzzles you. Similarly, the solution you craft today might help a co-worker with a similar situation tomorrow.

Never Leave Them Hanging

I'd been trying to get a training contract with a particular school district. Finally, they called asking if my company offered basic SharePoint training. Although we didn't normally offer that type of training, I really wanted their business and knew a trainer who could teach it. The school district ended up awarding us the contract for the project, but upon further discussion, I realized that they were looking for training that was beyond our level of competency, so I told them that we weren't the right company for their project. The school district was very angry, but I didn't understand why; I was doing the right thing by turning down a project that we were not qualified to perform. I spoke with my business consultant who told me that I needed to fulfill the obligation since I'd already agreed to provide the service, even if it meant contacting a competitor to deliver the training. The problem was that I left my client hanging with no alternative.

When you have to say no, always offer an alternative.

DEALING WITH DIFFICULT
END USERS AND CUSTOMERS

There are actually very few genuinely difficult users and customers in the world. You might be thinking, "You don't know the users and customers in my workplace!" However, the majority of users and customers in the world are reasonable people. They may not think, look, or sound the way that you or I do. However, they are our users and customers, and it is our job to deal with them. They may get "difficult" from time to time, especially when they feel they've been let down. It's how we handle them that will determine if they continue to be a problem, or if we can turn them around.

Difficult situations and angry users and customers usually occur because some part of our core service has failed, or the customer or user perceives it to have failed. We have not delivered on time; the customer has the wrong product; it doesn't work; or it's not what the user expected. What happens next is that our customer or user comes to the interaction with us in a negative or angry frame of mind. It's what happens next that will decide whether they deal with us again or complain about us to other people. Remember, anger is a natural, self-defensive reaction to a perceived wrong. If there is a problem with our company's product or service, some frustration and disappointment is probably justified and understandable.

The trick is not just to concentrate on fixing the core service issues. Telling the user that we'll replace the product, deliver it in half an hour, or change the system so the problem will never happen again, may not be possible. It does not help to give this answer if we cannot fulfill it. Sometimes, we may not have an answer, and the end user or customer is going to hear "no."

When Someone is Abusive, Aggressive, or Threatening

I don't think there's ever a reason to tolerate someone who is abusive, aggressive, or threatening. Nor would I tolerate someone who is cursing at me. Fortunately, most people, even when they're very angry, don't engage in that type of behavior.

Discuss with your supervisor ahead of time how to handle those rare situations when a caller gets way out of line.

Here are two ways to handle such a situation:

- Maintain your calm. Say to the caller, "I'm going to transfer you to my supervisor." and make the transfer. Be sure to alert your supervisor before he or she picks up the transferred call.

- Maintain your calm. Say to the caller something like this, "I want to help you. I'm sorry this happened to you, but I'm not going to allow myself to be threatened or verbally abused. If it continues, I will disconnect." If you have to disconnect, make sure to immediately inform your supervisor.

Think about this ahead of time. Different people have different levels of tolerance for such behavior in other people. Try to figure out where your limit is before you encounter situations like this.

WHY SOME SITUATIONS GO WRONG

We Seem Like We Don't Care

Support situations can fail when we don't sound or act as if we care, are concerned or appreciate the customer's or end user's situation. Maybe we actually do care, but in order to convey our caring, we've got to choose compassionate and empathetic words and phrases that show we care. No one can read another's mind. Try saying things like:

- "I know this is very frustrating."

- "I'm sure I would feel the same way if I were you."

- "I am so very sorry."

- "If there was anything at all that I could do, believe me, I would."

Or try an honest expression of sympathy, saying something like, "I'm so sorry that happened to you." It's amazing how much of a calming effect that can have.

We Don't Listen

Too often, we try to jump in with solutions and don't allow our end users and customers to vent their feelings. We need to show the customer or end user that we're listening by what we say and how we say it. Understand that obnoxious users and customers are often embarrassed because they've made a mistake and want to blame it on someone, perhaps you. Showing that we're interested in what they have to say often helps us establish rapport with the other person. Active listening techniques, including asking to make sure you understand what they have said can go a long way toward fostering a good situation. By saying, "Let me make sure I understand what you said," you are reaching out to the user and showing you care.

We Let the User Upset Us

It is easy to allow the customer's or user's attitude to irritate or annoy us. The user picks up on this through our tone of voice and use of language, or our silence, and this fans the fire. Make it a game or challenge to see how many upset users and customers you can turn around. Don't take upset users' and customers' ranting and raving personally. (Admittedly, that can be easier said than done, but it's critical for success in emotionally charged support situations.) Don't get emotionally hooked. When we let users and customers "push our buttons," we lose. When we respond emotionally with anger, sarcasm, or blame, we can't respond rationally. When things heat up, cool off by saying that you need to research the situation and possible solutions, and ask if you may get back to your user or customer at a later time.

We Use the Wrong Words

Some trigger words cause users and customers to become more difficult: like "can't," "you'll have to," or a flippant "sorry about that." Be sure to offer users and customers an alternative. Choices provide users and customers some say in how they want to proceed. Instead of saying "I don't know," try "Let me get you an answer," or "Let me find out for you."

We Focus on Ourselves Instead of Seeing It from Another's Point of View

Maybe you think the customer or end user is making too much out of a small issue (and maybe, by your standards, they are). The point is that if the issue, whatever it is, seems like a big deal to the customer or end user, it is a big deal, regardless of how we might feel about it. We must always look at customers or end-users issues from their perspectives, just the same as we would want a customer service rep who's helping us to try to see our problem from our perspective. No matter what, it is a big deal for our users or customers, and they want us to acknowledge that.

WHAT HAPPENS WHEN WE MAKE A MISTAKE?

End users and customers will often judge the level of our service based on how well we recover from a difficult situation, and they are very likely to forgive us when we do it well. Difficult situations or "screw-ups" are opportunities to win supporters for life. Everybody makes mistakes. The way we deal with our mistakes communicates who we really are.

If our actions show people that we truly care about them and their needs, and that we dislike having to say "no" to their requests, we all win! They will walk away knowing that even though we had to decline their request, we tried everything in our power to give them what they wanted. They will appreciate us and show us courtesy in return.

INTERACTIVE EXERCISE:

Working Magic with End Users and Customers

This exercise is best done with a group of three or four, but you can certainly do it by yourself.

If you're in a group: Work through these scenarios together. Start by reading about the situation.

If you're working by yourself: Read through the scenario, then on a separate sheet of paper, write down your solution. It is often helpful to write down your solution one day, then revisit your solution a day or two later and see if you would change anything.

Whether you're in a group or by yourself, decide how you would approach the end user, and then write a script for what you would say to handle the situation.

Use your best communication skills to provide an answer for the end user.

1. A manager of the Sales Department calls and wants a contractor he has hired to have access to the corporate network. He is asking you for a special favor, even though it is company policy that only employees can have network access.

2. An end user calls to complain that when he walks away from his desk to attend meetings in the conference room, his network access times out, and he has to log in up to five times a day. He is frustrated, and wants you to change the timing on his computer to avoid being logged out of the system. You cannot reset the timing. This is a regulatory and security policy.

3. A project manager in a work group wants to set up a local share with her team. She is calling you to create permission for her to do this. You know that it is against company policy to set up permission for a local share.

4. It is company policy that no one can download and install software. A graphic designer has been waiting for six weeks to get a set of software DVDs required for her project, which is due next week. Her manager has approved the purchase order, but the software has not arrived. She wants to be able to download the trial version over the Internet to meet her deadline.

5. A software developer is putting together a project proposal for acquiring enterprise-wide software. He needs your help to investigate how this software will work with remote users on three different platforms. Your schedule is full, and your manager has just given you three tasks that you need to accomplish by Friday.

6.   A user complains that her computer is running slowly. Upon investigation, you find that she has many programs open at the same time.

7.   A department head wants you to take a look at his personal laptop because it's been running slowly.

8.   An upper-level executive wants you to help her add a stock ticker, streaming music, and Skype to her computer. Such programs can adversely affect network performance and are not permitted by policy.

FOR REFLECTION AND DISCUSSION

Think about the times when someone has told you "no" without offering an alternative or workaround. How did that make you feel?

Think about the times when someone has told you "no" and offered an acceptable alternative or workaround. How did that make you feel?

TO-DOS

Think of some of the requests your users or customers make of you where you have to say no. What are some possible alternatives or workarounds you can offer that might help solve their problem or issue?

Still thinking of the customer or user requests from the previous question, what are some of the language choices you could make to soften your responses?

What are some things you might do to prevent your customer or user from feeling like you left them hanging, even when you have to say no?

CHAPTER NINE:
STRESS MANAGEMENT

"Write your injuries in dust, your benefits in marble."

—Benjamin Franklin

Our jobs supporting end users or customers can be ridiculously stressful at times. Just ask any IT pro who's lost a mail server while an important negotiation was going on at his or her company, or ask a support rep at a bakery whose custom-prepared wedding cake got ruined in transit to the wedding! Even when disasters aren't happening, the stress continues. In this chapter, I'm going to help you identify your stress and deal with it. (No, this doesn't involve medieval torture devices for that certain user or customer.)

I've included some exercises to help you identify where your stress is originating and make decisions about whether to do something about it or just let it go.

Let's face it, supporting end users or customers can be one of the most stressful positions in all of business or IT because you face many of the same problems every day, but with different people. In this session, you'll learn practical, down-to-earth techniques for dealing positively with the inevitable stress of a support position:

- The impact of stress

- The stress management equation

- What's in your control—and what's not

- Personal stress activators

- You can influence the stress outcome

MANAGING YOUR STRESS

Stress is the body's nonspecific response to any demands made on it. It is the way our bodies react to our continually changing environment. Stress has physical and emotional effects on us and can create positive or negative feelings. The important thing to remember about stress is that certain forms of stress are normal and essential.

Why Some Stress Is Good For You

Many of us think of stress as a synonym for tension or pressure. Actually, stress is just the way we respond to change. Understanding stress and its effects can help you use it to your own advantage and turn potential sources of stress into positive challenges.

Eustress: Good Stress

Stress can be good when it helps us perform better or keeps us out of trouble. Certain forms and levels of stress keep us alert and productive. Stress can help us finish that paper that is due, complete the race when our resources are depleted, jump out of the way of a careening car, or answer a record number of support calls in a shift.

Good stress, also called *eustress*, arises from situations and events that we think of as positive but still trigger the stress response. These can include getting a promotion, graduating, starting a new job, moving, making more money, getting married, and even going on vacation. These good things are stressful because they involve a change in the way we act or think about things. Change is stressful, whether we label it good or bad.

Distress: Bad Stress

Stress is bad when it causes us to be upset or makes us sick (distress). Bad stress causes negative feelings, health problems, and lowers productivity. Once you have begun to experience the effects or symptoms of bad stress, you have gone beyond your optimal stress level.

Problems that arise that are beyond our control can, and often do, result in bad stress: a natural disaster that affects one's home, a baby spiking a fever in the middle of the night, layoffs at work, or an unexpected dental bill. Other times, the problems that cause us distress are within our control. Examples might include a bad work situation, high credit card balances, or toxic relationships.

Comparing Eustress to Distress

The body can't tell the difference between eustress and distress. Both can be taxing on the body. The key lies in how we deal with stress, either using it to enhance life or limit it. One stressor can cause both distress and eustress, too. For example, we often hear of how hardship builds character. Later in the book, you'll hear a story about a young woman who was incarcerated as a teen. Incarceration is certainly a stressor! The stress of the negative aspects of her incarceration is an example of distress. The stress of developing successful coping mechanisms to survive incarceration is an example of eustress.

Intensity vs. Duration

Understanding your stress level is important. If nothing in your life causes you any stress or excitement, you may become bored, depressed, or may not be living up to your potential. If everything in your life, or large portions of your life, causes you stress, you may experience health or mental problems that will make your behavior worse.

Recognizing when you are stressed and managing your stress can greatly improve your life. Some short-term stress—the feeling before an important job interview, test, presentation, or sporting event, may give you the extra energy you need to perform at your best. But long-term stress—constant worry over your job, school, money, or family – may actually drain your energy and deplete your ability to perform well. Such stress is low in intensity, but high in duration. Low-intensity/high-duration stress is that insidious stress that slowly eats away at us and can cause serious health problems and performance issues when left unchecked.

Short-term stress occurs when you find yourself under pressure in a particular situation. Short-term high-intensity stress helps you feel alert and alive. Sometimes, it can actually keep us alive! The rush of adrenalin helps you focus on the situation at hand. If you have had a near-miss while driving a car, you have likely experienced short-term high-intensity stress. Athletic competitions, academic or career tests, or even a chess game can cause high-intensity/low-duration stress. We recover from this type of stress fairly quickly, it can provide the extra burst of energy needed to complete a task, and rarely does it cause lasting problems. This kind of stress can, in fact, be your ally.

Stress Management Equation

Author and speaker Paul Senness created this simple, but effective stress management equation: A + B = C, where A represents your stress activators, B represents your personal beliefs and/or behaviors, and C represents your personal consequences. For example, let's say that one of your stress activators is conflict. Your personal belief is to confront conflict aggressively. Suppose that you have a conflict (A) with your boss. Because your personal belief (B) is to stand up for yourself and your personal behavior (B) is to confront conflict aggressively, you stand up to your boss, tell her that she's an idiot, and slam the door as you storm out of the office. Your personal consequence (C) could well be that you'll lose your job.

Consider this alternative: You have a conflict (A) with your boss. After losing your last job because of your personal behavior (B) to confront conflict aggressively, you decided to keep your personal belief (B) to stand up for yourself, but to modify your personal behavior (B) by respectfully saying to your boss that you disagree with her and asking her to help you understand her position. Your personal consequence (C) now could be to win the respect of your boss, resolve the source of stress, and keep your job.

Physical and Mental Signs of Stress

You've heard before that recognizing when you are under stress is the first step in learning how to deal with your stress, but what does that mean? Sometimes, we are so used to living with stress that we don't know how to identify it.

Whether you are experiencing short-term or long-term stress, your body and mind may be showing the effects. The following list shows some examples of stress activators. You probably have some of your own that may be different from those in the list, and some of the stressors in the list may not bother you at all. The key here is to know yourself well enough to know the things that cause you stress.

Stress Activators

- Conflict
- Impossible deadlines
- Regulatory environment
- Ambiguity

- Disorganization
- Water-cooler politics
- Change
- Lack of resources

We all have sets of beliefs that guide our behavior. In the following two lists, you'll see contrasting sets of beliefs. Some people's sets of beliefs fall entirely in one group or the other. Other people's sets of beliefs may include items from both lists.

PERSONAL BELIEF SET A

- It's a black-and-white world.
- You're either with me or against me.
- You've got to stand your ground no matter what.
- Other people need to understand where I'm coming from.

PERSONAL BELIEF SET B

- The world is comprised of varying shades of gray.
- You and I may not agree on everything. We both understand that there are often several correct paths to a destination.
- As we receive new information, sometimes a course correction is necessary.
- Remember Stephen Covey's wisdom, "Seek first to understand, then to be understood."

In the same way that we all have sets of beliefs that guide our behavior, we tend to follow those beliefs with certain sets of behaviors. As with the lists of beliefs, some people always exhibit behaviors from one list or the other, while other people exhibit behaviors from both lists.

PERSONAL BEHAVIOR SET A	PERSONAL BEHAVIOR SET B
• Get in your face and tell you what I think.	• Respectfully say I disagree with you and ask you to help me understand your position.
• Work long hours without saying anything and think of yourself as a martyr.	• Document your hours, discuss the workload with your boss, and ask how best to deal with the problem.
• Gossip about the boss and your co-workers, spread the latest rumors you hear.	• Inform yourself as to the facts of the various issues facing your organization and stop spreading gossip and innuendo.
• Agree to everything, but do nothing (passive aggressive behavior).	• Meet with your boss or co-worker, respectfully and professionally explain the issue(s) you have with what you have been asked to do, and ask for help in finding ways to resolve those issues.
• When faced with a lack of necessary resources, make arbitrary decisions about where to cut corners, disregarding the effect on quality.	• Ask your boss for help in deciding what to cut due to the lack of resources.

After reviewing the two sets of beliefs and behaviors, consider which sets of beliefs and which set of behaviors will most likely have a positive outcome for all parties involved, have a positive effect on your career, and most likely gain you the most respect from your boss and co-workers.

If you identified personal belief and behavior set B as the set most likely to produce a positive outcome, you're well on your way to personal happiness and career success. If you identified personal belief and behavior set A as the best way of thinking about things and dealing with stress, you may want to rethink your paths to personal happiness and career success.

Keep your mind open to new ways of looking at things and new ways of reacting to the things that happen to you. Bear in mind that just because something is new doesn't mean it is better, and just because something is old does not mean it is better. Similarly, just because something is new does not mean it is bad, nor just because something is old does not mean it is bad.

"Don't believe everything you think." (Kida 2006)

—Thomas E. Kida

"Fifteen hundred years ago everybody knew the Earth was the center of the universe. Five hundred years ago, everybody knew the Earth was flat, and fifteen minutes ago, you knew that humans were alone on this planet. Imagine what you'll know tomorrow."

—Agent K in *Men in Black*

SOUNDTHINKING POINT:
Put a Stop to Gossip

I was waiting for my turn in a local store and the person ahead of me was saying terrible things about another person in our community including accusations of adultery. She even said she didn't have first-hand knowledge, but was just repeating things she'd heard. I wonder how she would feel if someone were to say such things about her. She was potentially ruining another human being's reputation based on rumor and hearsay. Make it your practice to stop gossip. When someone starts sharing gossip with you, say things like "I really don't want to hear gossip, so please don't share it with me. I certainly hope no one ever spreads unfounded rumors about me." Make it your practice to always speak well of other people or don't say anything at all.

Stress Warning Signals

This list shows some common warning signs that stress may be affecting your body and mind:

- Tiredness
- Increased frequency of colds
- Chest pains or rapid heart rate
- Short temper or irritability
- Lack of concentration or inability to focus
- Upset stomach or indigestion

- Feeling on edge
- Anxiety
- Depression
- Boredom
- Insomnia
- Long-term health conditions

If you're experiencing any of these signals, especially on an on-going basis, something is not right in your life. Whether it is stress or something else, the above signals are warning signs telling you that something is wrong. Whether you deal with it personally or by seeking help, it is important to deal with it early. Untreated, stress can lead to serious health problems.

PERSONAL EXERCISE:
Dealing Positively with Your Stress

On a piece of paper, make four columns. In the first column, write down some of the things that cause you to feel stress, the stress activators. In the next column, indicate whether the stress is high-intensity/low-duration or low-intensity/high-duration. In the third column, indicate whether the stress is under your control or beyond your control. Focus on the stress activators that are low-intensity/high-duration and under your control. In the fourth column, write down your ideas about how to resolve the stress. As you think about possible solutions, there may be several that come to mind, or there may be one that just jumps out at you. Regardless, take several days to reflect on your solutions before deciding on a course of action. As you reflect, consider how to create a positive outcome for everyone involved. It may not be possible to please everyone with your decision, so focus on creating a positive outcome, not hurting other people unnecessarily, and being honest and forthright with everyone involved.

SOUNDTHINKING POINT:
When a Change Causes Another Person Pain

Sometimes, it may not be possible to make life changes without hurting another person. An example is when it's necessary to end a relationship. The key is to handle the change respectfully, honestly, and with kindness. Follow Meryl Runion's sage advice: "Say what you mean. Mean what you say. Don't be mean when you say it." (Runion 2010)

Often, we can deal positively with stress by simply recognizing its source and choosing a different response from past responses.

It is very important to recognize that there are some sources of stress that we can't control. When we have no control over a source of stress, our best choice is to simply let it go.

The Serenity Prayer

God grant me the serenity
to accept the things I cannot change,
courage to change the things I can,
and wisdom to know the difference.

For example, if you are stuck in a traffic jam with no way out, as frustrating and as maddening as it seems, there's nothing you can do about it. You can choose your reaction and still get to your destination at the same time, regardless of whether you choose to get angry and upset or to simply accept it and listen to your favorite music on the radio or an audio book. If you choose to get angry and upset, you'll introduce more stress into your life, potentially causing stress-induced illness or other negative outcomes. If you choose to accept that you cannot change the current situation, you can also choose to create a calm, serene experience for yourself as you wait for the traffic to clear. Your reaction is completely your choice.

THE STRESS MANAGEMENT TOOL

Another way to help manage your stress is with the Stress Management Tool. On a piece of paper, draw a large circle, leaving about an inch from the edge of the paper. Inside the large circle, draw a smaller circle, leaving about an inch between the outer ring and the inner ring.

Between the edge of the paper and the outer ring, write down your personal stress activators (A). Make a copy of the page with your stress activators. Now, on the original page, between the outer and inner rings, write down some of your personal beliefs and behaviors (B) that you use to deal with your stress activators. In the small circle in the middle (the bullseye), write down some of your personal consequences (C) from your personal beliefs and behaviors.

Now, on the copy of the page, start in the bull's-eye and write down your desired personal consequences or outcomes (the things you would ideally like to have happen). Next, in the middle ring, write down the new beliefs or behaviors that you can use to deal appropriately with the stress in your life.

YES, I'M STRESSED— NOW WHAT?!

Everyone has the freedom to choose his or her response to any situation. Freedom to choose is a condition of the mind; liberty is a condition of the environment. How many of the items that you listed do you have some control or choice over?

You can choose to be proactive and work at approaching stressors with a different attitude. You can try to accept those things that at the present you can't control, while focusing your efforts on the things that you can change.

Change your vocabulary from "If I only had" to "I can be ..." Focus on changing from the inside-out. Try using a different approach and, by being different, to effect a more positive change in what's outside of yourself.

Dealing with Stress

One of the most immediate and easiest ways to deal with stress is responding to your body's physical symptoms. Sometimes, this can be as easy as stopping what you're doing and taking a few deep, relaxing breaths.

- *Are irate callers getting on your nerves?* Go into another room, or even the bathroom or closet if you need to get away! Shut the door. Experience the quiet. Take a few deep breaths. Feel the tension go out of your head, neck, and shoulders.

- *Have you had another bad day with your boss or co-worker?* Walk down the hall, rinse your face in cool water in the bathroom, or head outside and walk around the block. Just getting away for a few minutes can be calming and help you relax.

- *Have you spent too long sitting at your computer?* Push back from your desk. Roll your head and shoulders. Rub your hands together quickly to warm them and place them over your weary eyes, or just close your eyes and let your face and neck relax. Breathe in and out slowly and deeply.

- *Do you need a shoulder to cry on?* Do you have someone you can talk to about what's happening in your life? Having someone you can share both the good and bad with is important.

- *Laugh.* Nothing relieves the tension in your body, or your mind, like a good laugh. Go find a funny video on YouTube. For starters, check out the break videos playlist on the soundtraining.net YouTube channel: *http://tinyurl.com/donsfunnyvideos*.

- *Find a distraction.* Join a group or organization where people share your interests. Take up a new hobby.

- *Are you too focused on your problems?* Get outside of your own problems. There are bigger issues in the world. Choose an issue that you care about and donate time and energy working to overcome it. When you are busy helping others, your problems seems smaller. If you find yourself feeling sorry for yourself and your circumstances, think about what it must be like living on the street, in a war-torn area, or an area of the world suffering from famine or drought. Suddenly, things may not seem so bad.

Whether you start to take yoga classes, decide to organize your finances, get a massage, take up meditation, start a prayer life, start golfing (Some golfers say golf can be stressful!), or go to a comedy club with a friend to help you deal with stress, you have options. Stress can seem overwhelming. Stress can be isolating. But you are not alone, and you can minimize stress and make it work for you.

The Importance of Breathing

No matter how you choose to deal with your stress, it is important to understand the power of controlled breathing. Normally, we breathe in short, shallow breaths. When you find yourself in a stressful situation or when you simply want to relax for a moment, try controlled breathing. Sit on the edge of your chair, back straight, with your hands in your lap or resting on your knees. Close your eyes, if you wish. Breathe in through your nose to a count of five and exhale through your nose to a count of five. Repeat five times (or more, if you like).

Create a Get Out of Stress Free Card

Take a blank sheet of paper or an index card and pin it to your wall or keep it in an easily accessible place. Jot down things that make you feel peaceful and happy. You can also paste small pictures of people, places, and things that make you feel peaceful and happy. When you find yourself feeling stress, take a minute and look at this card.

WHAT ABOUT DIET?

This may be overly simplistic, but it's certainly true that our bodies are like a car. If we put bad gasoline in our car, it won't run well, and if we put bad food in our bodies, they won't perform as well as when we feed them wholesome, nutritious food. A diet rich in sugars (either natural or artificial), processed foods, and high-fat content foods can lead to a long list of problems, including heart disease, cancer, obesity, and impaired cognitive abilities. There's a joke among IT people that "if it doesn't come out of a vending machine, it's not food." Unfortunately, as with many jokes, there's a lot of unfortunate truth to it. Consider modifying your diet to include fresh fruits and vegetables, fish, whole grains, and water and avoid processed foods with high sugar or fat content, like drive-thru burgers and soft drinks. Remember to follow the recommendation we've all heard about drinking eight eight-ounce glasses of water per day.

As always, do your own research and talk with a dietitian, nutritionist, or a medical professional for the most current and accurate information on dietary concerns.

The following are good sources of information about nutrition:

- The U.S. Department of Health and Human Services Dietary Guidelines (*www.health.gov/dietaryguidelines/2010.asp*)

- The Academy of Nutrition and Dietetics (*www.eatright.org*)

- The Institute of Medicine (*www.iom.edu*)

- The Mayo Clinic (*www.mayoclinic.com*)

FOR REFLECTION AND DISCUSSION

What are the things that cause you to feel stress? What can you do about them?

As tough as your own challenges are, there are probably other people in the world facing and overcoming much greater challenges. Read the stories in chapter ten about people who persevered and overcame their challenges. Then, come back to this reflection point and see if your perspective has changed.

Think of someone you know who seems to rarely be affected by stress. Do you notice any differences between how she or he deals with stressful situations and how you deal with similar situations?

Do you ever find yourself worrying about things over which you have no control? Can you think of ways to accept those things in your life?

To-Dos

Create a Get Out of Stress Free card

Make a list of the things you eat during the day. If your diet consists of a lot of processed foods, artificially flavored or sweetened drinks, or high-fat content foods, consider modifying your diet to include more fresh fruits and vegetables, whole grains, fish, and water. Pay particular attention to the amount of water you drink every day. We've all heard the recommendation to drink at least eight eight-ounce glasses of water per day.

Enroll in a yoga class, an exercise class, or a meditation class.

Go for a walk in the park.

Volunteer at a homeless shelter.

Volunteer as a mentor for a high school student.

Listen to calming music.

CHAPTER TEN

OVERCOMING OBSTACLES

"Do the kinds of things that come from the heart. When you do, you won't be dissatisfied, you won't be envious, you won't be longing for somebody else's things. On the contrary, you'll be overwhelmed with what comes back."

—Morrie Schwartz (Albom 1997)

I want to tell you stories about five people who faced seemingly insurmountable challenges. These stories are about how these ordinary people dealt with extraordinary barriers.

The Importance of Education

Defying the Taliban

In 2012, Malala Yousafzai was a fifteen-year old Pakistani school girl who had achieved international fame by blogging about her efforts to attend school and obtain an education in a part of the world where the Taliban had imposed strict Sharia law. On October 9, 2012, several gunmen boarded her school bus, identified her, and shot her in the head for having the audacity to pursue an education and blog about it. She survived and was airlifted to Great Britain where her story continues to inspire people globally.

On July 12, 2013, her sixteenth birthday, Malala addressed the United Nations Youth Assembly and called on world leaders to protect rights to equality and education.

Malala and her family believe so strongly in the importance of education and the acquisition of knowledge that they put their lives on the line in support of their principles.

To find out more about Malala, there are many online resources devoted to her, including a Wikipedia page and a Facebook page.

Defying the Odds

Starcia Ague's mother kicked her out of the house when she was eleven. She went to live with her dad, who cooked and sold methamphetamine. She started a college fund for herself by charging his customers a surcharge to see him. She lost her college fund when he was busted and the authorities confiscated all the cash in the house. After the bust, she lived with relatives and friends for a while, eventually landing back with her mother. Starcia was fifteen when she was adjudicated delinquent and convicted of, among other things, masterminding a home invasion. She was sentenced to a juvenile detention facility where she would remain until she turned twenty-one.

The odds were not in Starcia's favor.

While she was in jail, at the age of sixteen, she heard a woman speak whose life had been even more difficult than hers. Starcia thought if this woman could make it, she could, too. She began to work on turning her life around.

She realized that education and a belief in a higher power were the rocks she needed to change her life. From the beginning, she knew it was not going to be easy. She asked the authorities at the juvenile facility about her transcripts and educational opportunities. She was met with distrust and laughter, but another youth in the facility had been successful in pursuing an education. That served as inspiration and motivation for Starcia to do the same. Again, the authorities rebuffed her, but she persevered, writing letters to college presidents and other influential people. Eventually, her tenacity paid off and she was able to complete not only her high school diploma, but also an associate's degree, all while she was incarcerated.

Upon her release on her twenty-first birthday, she applied to Washington State University, eventually earning a bachelor's degree in Criminal Justice. She intended to work with incarcerated youth, but because of her prior convictions, even though they occurred when she was a minor, she was prohibited from doing so. Again, using her innate resourcefulness, she pursued and was successful in obtaining a full and unconditional pardon from the governor, the only juvenile in the history of Washington State to do so.

Starcia went from being a victim to being a victor.

In my 2013 interview, when she was twenty-five, I asked Starcia how she motivates herself, how she gets herself up when she gets in a funk. She said she thinks about how far she's come and how there are so many people who've had it worse than she. She also thinks about all the work that remains to be done to help juvenile offenders successfully integrate into society and looks forward to working toward that end.

I noticed during our interview that Starcia frequently expresses gratitude for the people who've been her supporters. She doesn't seem to take anything for granted.

Starcia believes that the answer is never "no" for her. She just has to find another way around. Today, she works to help kids who are going through the juvenile justice system. She has a website at _www.starciaague.org_ where she creates awareness of issues facing juvenile offenders as they work to re-enter society and become productive citizens.

Your Challenge

What would you be willing to do to acquire more education and knowledge? What are the things you think are so important that you'd risk your life for them?

Are you willing to keep trying, through tenacity, perseverance, and sheer force of will to achieve something you believe in for yourself and the important people in your life?

LETTING GO OF ANGER, BITTERNESS, AND RESENTMENT

Escape from North Korea

I recently met a young woman who escaped from North Korea. Myeonghee Kim's father was killed for the food he was trying to bring to his family and her mother died from cancer because there was no medical care available. She and her sister faced the choice of staying in North Korea and almost certain death from starvation or trying to escape and possibly getting killed in the process. They made three attempts to escape, finally succeeding on the last one. Her sister fell into the grip of human traffickers in China and was forced into marriage. They had no contact with each other for nine years, until they were finally able to reconnect.

Today, she and her sister are citizens of South Korea, and she is in the United States as part of a Korean American exchange program. She is a very positive, upbeat, kind, and happy person who's a delight to be around.

How does your life compare to hers in North Korea?

Your Challenge

Can you stop every day to express gratitude for the gifts you've been given in your own life?

Surviving the Chinese Cultural Revolution

Manchung Ho was a child, living in the Chinese city of Guangzhou and studying the violin when Chairman Mao instituted the Chinese Cultural Revolution. In 1971, during the peak of the anti-Soviet period, China had enacted a motion to move all untrustworthy Communist people out of the city, which was called the Dispersion Act. Manchung and his family were forced to leave their home in Guangzhou and move to their ancestral village, even though no one from their family had lived there for three generations. In the village, there were no teachers available, so Manchung had to stop playing music. He and his siblings were expected to work the farms after school. Three years later, the communist party realized the policy was a mistake and Manchung's family was called back to the city of Guangzhou. Manchung was able to play the violin again for propaganda programs in high school. Although he resumed studying violin, his teachers were reluctant to teach standard Western repertoire because it was considered a capitalist art form.

After a decade, the disastrous experiment called the Cultural Revolution ended and Manchung and his family moved to Hong Kong. Manchung started his formal musical education in his mid-20s, which is considered a late start for a musician.

Manchung later came to the United States to attend graduate school, studying violin performance. Today, he is a successful music teacher and professional musician.

I've known Manchung for fourteen years. He could have allowed his experiences during the Cultural Revolution to ruin the rest of his life through bitterness and resentment. Instead, he is philosophical about his experience. He certainly could be bitter, but he's not. He is always happy, positive, upbeat, and hopeful about the future.

He reminded me in a recent conversation that he must never forget what happened during the Cultural Revolution, but he refuses to allow it to define who he is today and in the future.

Your Challenge

Did something happen to you in the past that still haunts you today? Do you feel anger or bitterness about what happened? When we permit it, anger, bitterness, and resentment can hold us in a crushing grip, hijacking our lives to no positive end.

The cruel paradox is that anger, bitterness, and resentment hurt only the person harboring those feelings and the friends and family members close to him or her. They have no effect on the people from the past who may have caused us pain or difficulty.

It's a choice. Can you let go of anger, bitterness, and resentment to allow yourself a life of happiness and hope?

KNOWING THE LIMITS OF YOUR POWER

Surviving a Cancerous Double-Play

Steve Edmiston is a successful attorney, screenwriter, and filmmaker in Seattle. He is married and a father of two college-age kids. He is active as a youth leader in his church.

In July of 2007, during an unrelated medical test, his physician noticed an anomaly that turned out to be Hodgkin's lymphoma. His physician said, "If you're going to get cancer, this is the one to get because it's fairly easy to cure." He went through six months of chemotherapy and was in remission for six months. Then, the cancer returned. He went through more chemotherapy, but his body didn't respond appropriately and his prognosis changed from hopeful to much less so. His doctors implemented an experimental therapy regimen, which was ultimately successful. In January of 2010, he had a stem cell transplant using cells from his own body, which was also successful. As of this writing, in the summer of 2013, he is still cancer free.

I asked Steve how he dealt with his cancer journey. He said the experience changed how he looks at life challenges. In some circles, it's popular to talk about fighting the cancer. People will say, if you fight hard enough, you can beat it, which implies that dying from cancer is a result of not fighting hard enough. He believes it's important to understand this: You must do what you need to in response to the cancer, but the notion that you actually have control is an incredible burden to put on the patient. There are some patients who are incredible fighters who are not going to win, and it's not their fault.

If you'd like to know more about the idea of successfully living with cancer, visit *http://www.cancersupportcommunity.org*.

Dealing with a Recession

In 2008, when the economy took a big downturn, my business slowed to a crawl. Some of my best competitors went out of business.

For the first few months of the slowdown, I fretted and worried about the future. Then, it dawned on me that some things are out of my control. I realized that my responsibility was to do everything necessary and possible for the care and feeding of my business. I was not, however, responsible for fixing the global economy nor putting money in the budgets of my clients so they could contract with me for projects.

I checked with Janet, my wife, to make sure she would stick around. I was pretty sure she would, but I was feeling a little insecure at the moment. She assured me she would.

I realized that the worst thing that might happen would be that we would lose a bunch of the stuff we owned, including the possibility of losing our house. We had a fair amount of money in savings, so that was only a remote possibility.

Then, I thought about how, whenever the economic slowdown ended and business picked back up again, I didn't want to look back at the slow period and think about all the things I could have done with all that free time.

I made sure to do the things necessary for my business and I also started pursuing some of the activities I'd been saving for retirement. I'd taken a lot of theatre and acting classes in high school and college, so I auditioned for and was cast in several plays and films. (I actually have my own IMDB page with two films listed.) I'd let my music take a distant backseat to other things for years, so I started studying pipe organ and vocal music again. I even got hired as music director at a church. That was not only fulfilling from a creative standpoint, it also replaced some of the lost income. I started writing books, like this one, and to my surprise and delight, people started buying them. My traditional business had slowed to a crawl, but I was having a great time discovering new sources of income and new ways to engage my creativity.

Thankfully, business gradually began picking up again, and I started getting busy with speaking engagements and training seminars. I've cut back on some of the activities I did during the slow times, but I look back and am very grateful I made the choices I made to take advantage of the unplanned free time and to live and enjoy my life.

I recognize that there are some things I can control and some things over which I have no control. I try never to worry about those things I can't control.

Occasionally, students will ask how to let go of worry about things beyond their control. It starts with how we view things and sometimes requires a mental shift. Cognitive therapists sometimes walk their clients through "What if?" scenarios to get them away from fears of a catastrophic outcome. In a way, that's what I did with myself as I thought through the worst possible outcomes from the decline in my business. I realized that the truly important parts of my life weren't going to change and the things I might lose were just stuff. Even my family home is just stuff, especially compared to having great relationships, health, food, and relative freedom.

Of course, I don't want to lose my stuff! I like my stuff and I'm proud of my business, so I'm always going to do everything possible to help my business prosper and keep my stuff. It's just that, at the end of the day, I have to recognize that some things are out of my control. Not only does it not do me any good to worry and fret about the things beyond my control, it can cause me to experience health and relationship problems. Such pointless worrying may actually take my focus away from thinking creatively about how to solve problems that are under my control.

I realized that, if I measure my net worth in dollars after the recession, I would see a string of failures. If, on the other hand, I measure my net worth in terms of great experiences and nurturing relationships, I would see a string of tremendous successes.

Your Challenge

Reflect on the things you worry about. Are there things over which you worry and fret that are beyond your control? Is it possible that such worrying and fretting is causing health and/or relationship problems elsewhere in your life? Might your worrying and fretting be keeping you from focusing creative energies on solving problems within your control?

PUTTING THINGS IN PERSPECTIVE

Sometimes, when I get self-absorbed and start to feel sorry for myself, I try to remember how fortunate I am. I live in a place where I'm relatively free to travel, go to school, and pursue my dreams. I'm not incarcerated, my family is fairly normal, my children are healthy and well-adjusted, the women in my life are able to work for women's rights and equality without fearing barbaric reprisals, and I don't need to worry about food or medical care. As crazy as I think some of our government leaders are, they're certainly not self-appointed dictators, nor successors to a throne, and they're not engaging in social engineering on the scale of the Chinese Cultural Revolution. Our system of checks and balances works pretty well.

What does this have to do with customer service or information systems and technology? When our bosses, end users, or customers are making us crazy or when our systems aren't behaving the way we want, just think about Myeonghee from North Korea. What would she have to say about our situation?

What would Manchung say? How would Starcia deal with it? What would Steve do? What would Malala say?

We all face challenges nearly every day. Everyone's challenges are different. Some are greater than others. Sometimes, our challenges may seem insurmountable, but most of us have never faced the types of challenges that confronted Malala, Myeonghee, Manchung, Steve, or Starcia.

When your challenges seem overwhelming, here are nine ways to knock them down to size:

- **Put things in perspective**. Compared to Malala facing death threats in Pakistan, Myeonghee facing starvation or possible execution, Manchung's experiences during the Chinese Cultural Revolution, Steve's second go-around with cancer, or Starcia facing a lifetime of struggle for a decision she made when she was thirteen, your challenges probably don't seem all that great.

- **Believe in the power of human perseverance and tenacity**. Keep looking for alternatives. If one path doesn't lead to a desired outcome, look for another one.

- **Break your challenge down into more easily digestible parts**. Sure, it's hard to see your way out of $100,000 in debt, but wouldn't it feel good to get it down to $99,000, then $98,000, and so on. The great writer Anne Lamott, in her book *Bird by Bird: Some Instructions on Writing and Life* says that's how to write a book, one word at a time (Lamott 1995).

- **Make a list**. When you're facing a seemingly overwhelming list of things to do, write them down. Knock out the quick and easy things first to trim down the list. The psychological effect of seeing a shorter list can be empowering.

- **Ask for help**. Ask anyone for anything to help. The answer's always "no" until you ask. When I'm traveling, I shamelessly ask for upgrades from airlines, hotels, and rental cars. Sometimes, I get them, but I'd never get them if I didn't ask.

- **Reward yourself** with words of affirmation as you start to tear down the walls that block you. Be your own cheerleader, even if you don't feel like it. Just go through the motions. Say the words "Way to go" or "Good job." The mere fact of saying positive words can also be empowering.

- **Give yourself grace**. Give yourself the grace to lose an occasional battle on the way to winning the war. Not everything you do is going to work. That's OK. If a particular tactic didn't work on overcoming your challenge, it certainly did work on letting you know what works and what doesn't. In golf, even the best pros hit bad shots. They allow themselves a moment of frustration (and sometimes profanity) in response to the bad shot. Then, they recover their composure and get on with the game. Life is a marathon with detours, slowdowns, and setbacks, not a sprint from start to finish.

- **Recognize that you can't control everything**. Some things are beyond your control. Make a list of the challenges you're facing. Divide the list into the things over which you have control and the things over which you have no control. Stop fretting over things you can't control. Prioritize the things you can control and start dealing with them.

- **Do an inventory of your blessings**. Everyone has been blessed with gifts, no matter how small or insignificant they may seem. It may be something as simple as a smile from a friend or the rain that brings us the lush vegetation of the Pacific Northwest. Pause and give thanks for your blessings. People who have an abiding sense of gratitude experience far fewer neurotic thought processes than those who don't.

Here's the great news about being human. Thanks to neuroplasticity, our brain's ability to adapt by forming new neural connections, each of us has the ability to grow, adapt, and make ourselves into the person we want to be, whether that's a matter of becoming even more of the person you already are or remaking yourself into a whole new person, it starts by recognizing that we can do it.

For Reflection

1.   Think about someone, other than yourself, who's beaten the odds.

2.   Think of someone, from your own life or someone else's, who has overcome adversity through perseverance and tenacity.

3.   Is there a big challenge facing you today that you can break down into smaller chunks?

4.   Have you ever been afraid to ask someone for something? What's the worst thing that would have happened if you had asked that person for help?

5.   What does grace mean to you?

6.   Name three things for which you're grateful.

7.   Are there things in your work or personal life that you can't control, but which still cause you to worry and fret. What good does it do to worry and fret over things you can't control? Can you think of ways to let go of those things that are beyond your control?

EPILOGUE

I would maintain that thanks are the highest form of thought; and that gratitude is happiness doubled by wonder.

—G. K. Chesterton (Chesterton 1917)

I n Japan, there is a form of meditation known as Naikan (pronounced like the Nikon camera brand). Naikan literally means "inside looking," or introspection. Naikan is about living a life filled with gratitude, and a vital aspect to becoming a compassionate geek—for in the presence of an abiding sense of gratitude, there's little or no opportunity for neurotic thought processes to develop.

In my own life, I've found that the times when I'm most self-absorbed and feeling a sense of entitlement are the times when I'm least happy and least able to be a contributing, productive member of society. Conversely, the times when I'm most aware of the tremendous gifts I've been given and most grateful for those gifts are the times when I'm the happiest and best able to make a difference in the lives of the people around me.

In the actual practice of Naikan, the compassionate geek reflects on three questions:

1. What have I been given (by my mother, father, aunts, uncles, grandparents, siblings, other relatives, friends, acquaintances, strangers)?

2. What have I given (to my mother, father, aunts, uncles, grandparents, siblings, other relatives, friends, acquaintances, strangers)?

3. What troubles or difficulties have I caused (my mother, father, aunts, uncles, grandparents, siblings, other relatives, friends, acquaintances, strangers)?

Upon reflection, we begin to realize that we're all living blessed lives. Certainly, some people have been more fortunate than others, but that's not the point. The point is that each of us has been given tremendous gifts. When we focus on our blessings instead of our injuries (real or imagined), we reframe our thinking toward a more positive, uplifting perspective. At the very least, this leads to a more pleasant life experience, and it can also help cure some illnesses and help us overcome adversity.

Don't believe me? Consider Alice Herz-Sommer, the world's oldest Nazi concentration camp survivor, who is 109 years old at the time of this writing. Not only did she survive the Theresienstadt concentration camp as a young mother, but she survived a bout with cancer in her 80s. She lives by herself in a flat in London and practices piano three hours every day. In a 2011 interview with Anthony Robbins, she said, "I always look for the good. I know there's bad, but I look for the good." (Herz-Sommer 2011) It's a choice she makes about how to view her world. She made that choice when she was in the concentration camp; she made it when she was diagnosed with cancer; and she makes that choice today.

All of the great wisdom traditions emphasize the importance of living a life of gratitude. The fourteenth-century Christian philosopher Meister Eckhart said, "If a man has no more to do … than be thankful, that would be enough." (Eckhart 2009) In his book Born for Love: Reflections on Loving, author Leo F. Buscaglia quotes his Buddhist teacher who would remind his students, "Let's rise and be thankful, for if we didn't learn a lot today, at least we may have learned a little. And if we didn't learn even a little, at least we didn't get sick. And if we did get sick, at least we didn't die. So let us all be thankful." (Buscaglia, 1994) It's truly all a matter of perspective. Suppose you're driving to work and you have a flat tire. Certainly, no one will blame you for getting upset, but the reality is that you still have to change the tire and get to work, whether you get upset or not. Either way, you'll arrive at work in about the same amount of time. The difference is that you can get angry and stressed out or you can pause for a moment and give thanks for the blessings of your life including the car and the set of tires that got you this far, the well-maintained road on which you traveled, and a generally civil society that allows you to travel without worrying about roadside bombs or similar dangers that affect people in some parts of our world. If you make the choice to get angry and stressed out, that's how you'll arrive at work and that's how you'll start your workday. If, on the other hand, you pause and reflect on your blessings, accepting the inconvenience of a flat tire, you'll arrive at work in a much better frame of mine, better prepared to take on the workday. It's purely a matter of perspective and it's entirely your choice how you choose to react to the things that happen to you.

When we're grateful for our customers, end users, colleagues, bosses, and everyone else around us, it makes it much easier to be kind, to show compassion, empathy, and respect, to be a good listener, to find ways to say "no" with finesse and grace, to manage the stress in our lives, and to overcome our personal adversity.

I want to end by saying how grateful I am for your investment of time and money in this book. I sincerely hope I've given you some helpful information along with some challenges and reflections to help you in your life's journey.

As Stewart Brand said in *The Whole Earth Catalog* and as Steve Jobs quoted in his Stanford University commencement address, "Stay hungry. Stay foolish." I'm going to add, stay awesome.

APPENDICES

APPENDIX A:
TEN WAYS TO DELIGHT YOUR END USER

As an IT support technician, you could very well be a hero to your user today! Your job is incredibly important, because you are often the bridge between where a user is on a project and where she or he wants to be. You even have the power to help your users have a great day by solving their problems and freeing them to think more creatively and be more productive in their jobs. There are many studies that have shown how well-trained IT support personnel add directly to a company's bottom line by helping employees work more productively and creatively. Here are ten simple and practical techniques you can put to use today to start making a positive difference in people's lives.

Respond Quickly

Quick responses can take several forms. Ideally, you simply answer the phone and solve the problem. Anyone who has spent any time in an IT support position knows that's not always possible, so what other options exist? Automated voice response systems that let callers know about how long they should expect to wait are great; email responses that do the same thing are also great. The key is to inform users and customers as to the approximate wait time until they get a response. Armed with accurate information, users can then make an informed decision as to whether to wait on hold or hang up and call back later. If they're communicating via email, they can make a decision about whether to wait for a response or move on to another project and return to the one requiring support at a later time.

First Impressions Count

Start the call or in-person visit with a pleasant, professional greeting, and for heaven's sake, be real! In other words, a simple, "Hello, this is Don Crawley. May I help you?" is far better than some contrived greeting like "Hello, this is Don Crawley. How may I provide excellent service to you today?" If your organization requires you to say specific words in your greeting, work on making them genuine. Nothing is worse than hearing someone answer the phone reading a script in a monotone voice or a condescending tone. When you're forced to use a standardized greeting, try to understand your employer's intent in requiring the standardized greeting. Even if you think the words you're required to say are phony, your employer's intent is not phony; your employer wants you to deliver excellent service, so find a way to believe it and mean it when you say it. Make it real!

Display Honest Competence

Tell callers that you'll either fix their problem, find someone who can, or find a workaround. No one has all the answers, and no one expects you to have all the answers. They do, however, expect you to be familiar with common troubleshooting techniques, to be honest about your abilities, and to be honest when you don't know the answer.

Reassure

Reassure your users that you're committed to solving their problems. Saying things like, "Tracy, I'm creating a file on this issue so I can follow up on it and make sure we solve it for you," assures your user that you're taking ownership of their problem. In fact, when you say those exact words, "I'm taking ownership of this issue," you tell your users that you're with them and that you're going to see the issue through to some sort of resolution, whether it's actually solving the problem, escalating it, or developing a work-around.

Keep It Positive

Focus on what you WILL do instead of what you WON'T do. Keep the
conversation upbeat, even when the user wants to complain about things
unrelated to the problem at hand. Your user doesn't want to hear you complain
about computers, Microsoft, the company, or any of the myriad things people
complain about. Dare to be different and avoid the temptation to join users in
their complaining.

Empathize

Empathize with your user. You can empathize without complaining. Use
empathetic statements like, "I don't blame you. I'd be frustrated too, if that
happened to me." Ross Shafer says people don't want customer *service* as much
as they want customer *empathy*. Imagine how you'd feel if you were under
deadline and a document failed to print. Imagine how you'd feel if you were
trying to get out the door and your computer locked up. Remember the three
S's: Keep it sincere, short, and then deliver a solution (or at least a workaround).

Be Gracious

Similar to empathy, graciousness helps endear you to users; it lets users know
you appreciate them and what they're going through in trying to do their job.
As you're working on their problems, thank them for calling and let them know
how much you appreciate the opportunity to help. (The reality is that when
they call and ask us to help, we can often head off bigger problems down the
road. We really DO appreciate the opportunity, because it can save us a lot of
time and frustration in the future!) As always, be careful to be sincere. People
can easily detect insincerity.

Be Respectful

Thanks to the mass media, our society has become disrespectful. It's not necessary to respect someone in order to treat them respectfully. In the movie *The Green Mile*, Tom Hanks' character treats condemned criminals on death row with respect. Certainly, persuasive arguments can be made that the condemned men with whom he dealt were not deserving of respect, but he treated them respectfully anyway. People tend to behave the way you expect them to. Often, the way you're treated is a mirror of how you treat others.

Offer One Bonus Tip

This could be something new that you've discovered in a widely used application, such as Microsoft Outlook or a new resource available on the company's network. Use good judgment on this; if your user is obviously in a hurry to get back to work, save your bonus tip for later. If, on the other hand, you've established rapport with your user, offer a bonus tip by saying something like, "By the way, Pat, we're letting everyone know about a way to color code appointments in Outlook. It's really easy and people seem to use it a lot once they know about it. Are you aware of this?"

Always Confirm Resolution

Always remember to confirm resolution of the problem or issue before hanging up the phone, leaving the user's or customer's workplace, or otherwise closing the ticket. Phrases to use include, "Have I solved your problem?" or "Does that take care of the reason for your call?" or "Is everything taken care of to your satisfaction?"

As with all things, be sensitive to your users' moods and circumstances. If they're obviously in a hurry or angry, avoid small talk and say something like, "I can tell you're in a hurry, so I'm going to be respectful of your time and just get to work on your problem" or "I can tell you're upset right now. I don't blame you at all, so I'm going to get right to work on solving this issue." Be sure to punctuate lengthy periods of silence with comments like, "I'm not ignoring you; I'm still working on this problem." If the person with whom you're dealing is technically sophisticated, you could even let him/her know what you're doing. If, on the other hand, the user is not technically sophisticated, just let him/her know that you're not ignoring them.

Above all, remember that our jobs in Information Systems and Technology are not about technology at all; they're about delivering creative solutions to workplace problems. Everything revolves around our users. We have to help them be more productive and creative in their jobs by helping them be more proficient with the tools of Information Systems and Technology.

Appendix B:
Recommended Reading

Don't Believe Everything You Think: The Six Basic Mistakes We Make in Thinking, Thomas Kida, Prometheus Books, 2006.

Emotional Intelligence: Why It Can Matter More Than IQ, 10th Anniversary Edition, Daniel Goleman, Bantam Dell, New York, New York, 2006.

Enchantment, Guy Kawasaki, Penguin Books, London, 2011.

How to Win Friends and Influence People, Dale Carnegie, Simon & Schuster; Reissue edition (November 3, 2009).

Man's Search for Meaning, Viktor E. Frankl, Washington Square Press, New York, 1959.

Social Intelligence, Daniel Goleman, Bantam Dell, New York, New York, 2006.

The Four Agreements, Miguel Angel Ruiz, M.D., Amber-Allen Publishing, Inc., San Rafael, California, 1997.

The Fred Factor, Mark Sanborn, Currency, 2004.

The Seven Habits of Highly Effective People, Stephen Covey, Free Press, New York, 1989.

Tuesdays with Morrie, Mitch Albom, Doubleday, New York, 1997.

Winners Never Cheat, Jon M. Huntsman, Wharton School Publishing, Upper Saddle River, New Jersey, 2005.

Appendix C:
Online Resources

Blog and Podcast: *www.compassionategeek.com*

Video Channel: *www.doncrawley.com/videos*

Facebook: *www.facebook.com/DonRCrawley*

Website: *www.doncrawley.com*

TED: *www.ted.com*

Kahn Academy: *www.khanacademy.org*

Center for Compassion and Altruism Research and Education: *http://ccare.stanford.edu/*

Charter for Compassion: *http://charterforcompassion.org/*

Empathy Bell Curve: *http://www.phikappaphi.org/forum/spring2011/ articles/pkpforum_spring2011_empathy.pdf*

Greater Good Science Center: *greatergood.berkeley.edu*

Mind and Life Institute: *http://www.mindandlife.org/*

Roots of Empathy: *http://www.rootsofempathy.org/*

BIBLIOGRAPHY

Albom, Mitch. 1997. *Tuesdays with Morrie*. New York, New York: Doubleday.

Bell, Daniel. 1980. *The Winding Passage*. Cambridge, Mass.: ABT Associates Inc.

Buscaglia, Leo F. 1994. *Born for Love: Reflections on Loving*. New York, NY: Ballentine Books.

Chesterton, G.K. 1917. *A Short History of England*. London: Chatto and Windus.

Covey, Stephen R. 2004. *The 7 Habits of Highly Effective People: Powerful Lessons in Personal Change*. Free Press.

Darley, J. M., and C.D. Batson. 1973. "From Jerusalem to Jericho": A study of Situational and Dispositional Variables in Helping Behavior". JPSP, 1973, 27, 100-108." *Journal of Personality and Social Psychology*.

Davich, Victor N. 2004. *8 Minute Meditation: Quiet Your Mind. Change Your Life*. Perigee Trade.

Eckhart, Meister. 2009. *The Complete Mystical Works of Meister Eckhart*. Translated by Maurice O'C. Walshe. New York: The Crossroad Publishing Company.

Frankl, Viktor E. 1959. *Man's Search for Meaning*. New York, New York: Pocket Books.

Goleman, Daniel. 2006. *Social Intelligence*: The Revolutionary New Science of Human Relationships. New York, New York: Bantam Dell.

Grice, Paul. 1989. *Studies in the Way of Words*. Cambridge, MA: Harvard University Press.

Herz-Sommer, Alice, interview by Anthony Robbins. 2011. *Everything is a Present* (October).

Hughes, Colonel Christopher P. 2007. *Conscience and Courage.* http://www.conscienceandcourage.org/index.php?page=6&issue=Vol4.

Kida, Thomas E. 2006. *Don't Believe Everything You Think.* Prometheus Books.

Lamott, Anne. 1995. *Bird by Bird: Some Instructions on Writing and Life.* New York: Anchor Books.

Le Boeuf, Michael Ph.D. 2000. *How to Win Customers and Keep them for Life.* New York: Berkley Books.

Luke. n.d. "The Gospel According to Luke." In *Holy Bible*, by Luke, 10:29-37.

Mayer, John D. 2005-2012. *Emotional Intelligence Information.* Accessed August 10, 2013. http://www.unh.edu/emotional_intelligence/ei%20What%20 is%20EI/ei%20what%20is%20home.htm.

Palmer, Harry. 1997. *Resurfacing: Techniques for Exploring Consciousness.* Star's Edge Creations.

Ricard, Matthieu. 2010. *Why Meditate? Working with Thoughts and Emotions.* Carlsbad, California: Hay House, Inc.

Runion, Meryl. 2010. *Power Phrases: The Perfect Words to Say it Right & Get the Results You Want.* Morgan James Publishing.

Sheikh Riyâd al-Musaymîrî, professor at al-Imâm University in Riyadh. n.d. http://en.islamtoday.net/node/635.

Zemke, Ron, Claire Raines, and Bob Filipczak. 1999. *Generations at Work: Managing the Clash of Veterans, Boomers, Xers, and Nexters in Your Workplace.* AMACOM.

INDEX

About Compassionate Geek

Compassionate Geek is a Seattle-area company specializing in people skills training for IT professionals, based on this book. Our online, on-demand training features videos, thought exercises, quizzes, reading, and more.

Review Compassionate Geek courses at *CompassionateGeek.com*

Subscribe to the Compassionate Geek blog at *CompassionateGeek.com/blog*

The Accidental Administrator®:

CISCO ASA SECURITY APPLIANCE

A Step-by-Step Configuration Guide

Your easy-to-follow guide to configuring a Cisco ASA Security Appliance from the ground up!

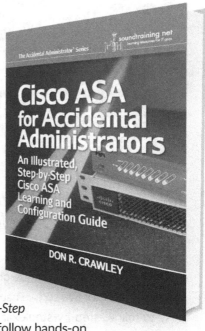

The Accidental Administrator: Cisco ASA Step-by-Step Configuration Guide is packed with 56 easy-to-follow hands-on exercises to help you build a working firewall configuration from scratch. Based on software version 8.3(1), it's the most straight-forward approach to learning how to configure the Cisco ASA Security Appliance, filled with practical tips and secrets learned from years of teaching and consulting on the ASA. There is no time wasted on boring theory. The idea is for you to be able to sit down with your ASA and build a working configuration in a minimal amount of time!

Designed to help you get a Cisco ASA up and running quickly!

BOOK DETAILS

Author:
Don R. Crawley

Categories:
Networking/Cisco

Distribution:
CreateSpace

Publisher:
Crawley International, Inc.
Auburn, WA
(206) 988-5858

Official release date:
August 3, 2010

Number of pages:
184

Book size:
7 x 9

ISBN:
978-1449596620

The Accidental Administrator®:

CISCO ROUTER STEP-BY-STEP CONFIGURATION GUIDE

Your easy-to-follow guide to configuring a Cisco router from the ground up!

Packed with interactive, hands-on exercises, loads of live screen captures, and easy-to-follow, step-by-step examples this guidebook helps you master your Cisco router. Applicable to all IOS-based routers, it's the most straightforward approach to configuring and managing a Cisco router. The essentials are covered in chapters on understanding TCP/IP, IP version 6, routing access-lists, NAT (network address translation) and more. There's no time wasted on boring theory, just loads of practical, down-to-earth advice, tips and techniques to help you master your Cisco router. Companion online videos make it even easier to understand and apply the knowledge.

Available in both paperback and Kindle editions!

BOOK DETAILS

Author:
Don R. Crawley

Categories:
Networking/Cisco

Distribution:
CreateSpace

Publisher:
Crawley International, Inc.
Auburn, WA
(206) 988-5858

Official release date:
September 25, 2012

Number of pages:
358

Book size:
8 x 10

ISBN:
978-0-9836607-2-9

The Accidental Administrator®:

LINUX SERVER STEP-BY-STEP CONFIGURATION GUIDE

Your easy-to-follow guide to configuring a Linux Server from the ground up!

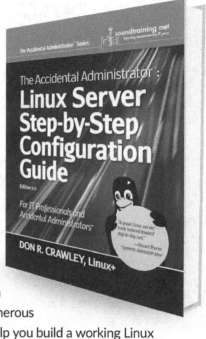

The Accidental Administrator: Linux Server Step-by-Step Configuration Guide is packed with 44 easy-to-follow hands-on exercises plus numerous command examples and screen captures to help you build a working Linux server configuration from scratch. It's the most straight-forward approach to learning how to configure a CentOS/Red Hat/Fedora Linux server (the book is based on version 5.4 and 5.5), filled with practical tips and secrets learned from years of teaching, consulting, and administering Linux servers. There is no time wasted on boring theory. All this information is presented in a straightforward style that you can understand and use right away.

Available in both paperback and Kindle editions!

BOOK DETAILS

Author:
Don R. Crawley

Categories:
Networking/Linux

Distribution:
CreateSpace

Publisher:
Crawley International, Inc.
Auburn, WA
(206) 988-5858

Official release date:
October 27, 2010

Number of pages:
188

Book size:
8 x 10

ISBN:
978-1453689929

TWEETING LINUX

140 Linux Configuration Commands Explained in 140 Characters or Less

A practical Linux command reference, complete with 164 screen captures and plain-language explanations

Tweeting Linux: 140 Linux Configuration Commands Explained in 140 Characters or Less is a straight-forward approach to learning Linux commands. Each command is first explained in 140 characters or less, then examples of usage are shown in screen captures, and finally more details are given when necessary to explain command usage. You'll see the most commonly-used commands, plus a few gems you might not know about. All information is presented in a straight-forward style designed for everyday use by working system administrators.

Available in both paperback and Kindle editions!

BOOK DETAILS

Author:
Don R. Crawley

Categories:
Computers/Operating
Systems/Linux

Distribution:
CreateSpace

Publisher:
Crawley International, Inc.
Auburn, WA
(206) 988-5858

Official release date:
August 24, 2011

Number of pages:
310

Book size:
5 x 8

ISBN:
978-0983660712

A COMPASSIONATE GEEK KNOWLEDGE GUIDE

THE 5 PRINCIPLES OF
IT CUSTOMER SERVICE SUCCESS

The 5 Principles of IT Customer Service offers a refreshing approach to IT customer service. Instead of prescribing rigid scripts and protocols, the reader learns how to live a more compassionate and empathetic life as a pathway to delivering exceptional customer service.

Available in print, Kindle, and Audiobook editions!

BOOK DETAILS

Author:
Don R. Crawley

Categories:
Communication
& Social Skills

Distribution:
C'Est Bon Press

Publisher:
Crawley International, Inc.
Auburn, WA
(206) 988-5858

Official release date:
September 11, 2016

Number of pages:
108

Book size:
5 x 8

ISBN:
978-0983660774

CPSIA information can be obtained
at www.ICGtesting.com
Printed in the USA
LVHW081926220822
726500LV00003B/161